More praise for *Getting Good Loving*

"Chapman explores the root causes of common problems between black men and women without using that knowledge as an excuse for destructive behavior. *Getting Good Loving* offers a positive approach to strengthen and encourage black couples rather than laying blame. I highly recommend this book to anyone seeking to better understand relationships between black men and women."

—Alvin Poussaint, M.D.

"With sensitivity and wit, [Chapman] suggests ways black men and women can shed their defenses and learn to trust each other again."

—*Publishers Weekly*

Getting Good Loving

ALSO BY AUDREY B. CHAPMAN

Man Sharing: Dilemma or Choice?

GETTING

GOOD LOVING

How Black Men and Women

Can Make Love Work

(Formerly entitled *Entitled to Good Loving*)

Audrey B. Chapman

Foreword by Marita Golden

ONE WORLD
Ballantine Books • New York

A One World Book
Published by Ballantine Books

This edition published by arrangement with Henry Holt and Company.

Due to the limitations of space, permissions appear on page 211.

Library of Congress Catalog Card Number: 95-94985

ISBN: 0-345-40245-6

Cover design by Kristine V. Mills
Cover illustration by Jose Ortega

Manufactured in the United States of America

First Ballantine Books Edition: January 1996

10 9 8 7 6 5 4 3 2 1

This book is dedicated to all the children in my family with all my love—Pamela, Christopher, Erik, Justin, Yinka, Asiatu, Diara, Jennifer, Scott, and Robin. It is also dedicated to any future children in the next generation. I hope the wisdon in this book will shed further light on love, expectations, and the solutions to any romantic difficulties, so that they may always find peace and happiness in their relationships.

Contents

Foreword

I think I'd better start with a warning: This book, if you let it, will change your life. Not just your love life, SISTER, BROTHER, but your *life* (which is where the love lives/hibernates/is camouflaged/or yearns to come out of the closet). In *Getting Good Loving*, Audrey Chapman brings the compassion and honesty that characterizes her radio show, articles, and earlier book to an examination of the often tangled terrain of the human heart.

The unique style that black men and women bring to the search for intimacy, the shaping of a marriage, the desire to love and be loved, has rarely been explored with more insight, commitment, and energy. Chapman transforms the blood, sweat, and tears of real black men and women into a narrative that is dramatic, informative, and inspiring. We've all been down the roads walked in these pages. Yet with Chapman as our guide, this time we don't get lost, and we find out not only where we've been but also where we're going.

As an African-American woman who thought my "stuff" was pretty tight, my "act" totally together, I nevertheless saw myself in the mirror once again while reading *Getting Good Loving*. Lessons historical and contemporary, revelations chilling and humorous, resonated much like the face of someone you love, the last good time you had, the dream you hold on to, days after I finished the book.

This discussion of the sociological and historical baggage black men and women bring with them and unpack in the bedroom, the dining room, on the job, and that sabotages so much of our real desire for love, is laced with a profound respect for and understanding of black men and women. If you're looking for an easy answer, a facile solution, someone to blame, close this book now. Audrey Chapman knows what our fantasies too often force us to forget: good loving ain't easy.

I should probably say now that Audrey Chapman changed *my* life, long before she wrote this book. Several years ago, in the midst of a deep period of doubt and depression about the absence of love in my life, I went to see Audrey Chapman. I poured out my heart and complained, like so many black women, about my propensity for finding or attracting men with whom I was incompatible or whom I loved but did not really like (dig *that!*). This was the state of *my* love life, despite a satisfying career, a son I loved, and a host of female friendships.

I'll never forget what Audrey Chapman told me in that first session: "Don't worry, we're going to get you so together 'those guys' won't even come near you anymore." Now, I'd done affirmations, and I *knew* prayer worked. But Chapman's certainty that my life would change made me shiver with anticipation and a little fear. What, I wondered, did she know that I didn't? Was she going to work roots? What Chapman did was help me to unleash—literally—my dormant capacity to love and trust myself, a force, that despite exterior signs to the contrary, was in actuality bruised and more than a little tattered. After several sessions I literally felt reborn. And I am here to testify that when Audrey and I got through working on me, "those guys"—you know the ones—were consistently deflected by some intangible force field of confidence that I began to radiate. I learned how to be friends with men, to appreciate them even if they didn't want to put a ring on my finger, and mostly how to value myself so much that I looked for a man the way I planned my career—with patience and discrimination, expecting and settling *only* for what I really wanted and needed.

Audrey Chapman believes happy endings are possible. She has helped hundreds of people find one. A year after I married the man I couldn't have met until she prepared me to, Audrey called my house one day and asked to speak to me. My husband answered the phone and, recognizing her voice, thanked her for helping me to do the work required for him to enter my life. I have thanked Audrey Chapman more than once and while I'm at it I think I'll say thanks one mo' again!

So, if you're married, turn off the television and read this book with your mate. If you want to be married, well, I told you what happened to me! If you're single, and afraid singlehood is a social death sentence, prepare to dance to the music of your unique self and love every minute of it and everything you are.

You will buy this book for sister friends and give it to the brother who listens as carefully to you as any of "the girls." But give it as well to the woman who says she has given up on men and the man who swears he'll never be "caught." Don't say a word, just give it to them. Send it Federal Express, or wrap it up pretty and put it on their desk, in their locker, or— if you want to get wicked—underneath their pillow. Believe me, they'll read it. Audrey Chapman may not work roots. But her words are filled with power. And she *knows* where the love is at.

—Marita Golden
November 1994

Acknowledgments

Expressing appreciation to those who have inspired us is especially appropriate in a book about loving ourselves and each other. There are many people to whom I am grateful for their support on this project.

This book could not have been written without the tireless dedication, wisdom, clarity, and encouragement of Judith S. Andrews, who collaborated in its writing. And a special thanks goes to her daughter, Mia, who learned to be patient and supportive by providing great meals for us in her home during the evenings when we worked well into the night. I am grateful to Betty Rothbart, M.S.W., for her amazing ability to function as a one-woman rescue squad and to assist so skillfully in the completion of the manuscript. And thanks to G. Sandra Goodson for her much-needed, last-minute secretarial help.

I gratefully acknowledge William Mayo, Joy Shelton, and Cherie Smith for their continued endorsement of this material. Appreciation also goes to Ronald Townes for his fine graphics. And I give special thanks to my friend Melvin L. Hardy, Jr., for all his help, advice, and computer assistance during the various crises that arose while working on the book.

I would also like to give thanks to my literary agent, Carol Mann, who provided tremendous guidance and advice on this project during the last several years. I am enormously grateful to my editor at Henry Holt, Theresa Burns, for her valuable contributions and time during many painful stages of the manuscript's development. Also thanks to assistant editor Tracy Sherrod, who was always there cheering me on.

Most important of all, I thank my clients and the many men and women who volunteered to share their personal stories so that others could understand their own relationships better; without them this book could not have been written. (The names, occupations, and residences of all those who appear anecdotally in this book have been changed to protect their privacy. Any resemblance of their circumstances or identities to persons living or dead is purely coincidental.)

Finally, my heartfelt thanks to all my dear friends and family members for putting up with my absences during this very intense period. Without their support and patience I could not have successfully completed this task so others might experience good loving.

Introduction

Relationship issues seem never to be far away from me. I was thinking this once while in line at a fast-food restaurant in downtown Washington, D.C., where many government workers gather. I was talking with another woman in line when I overheard several men and women involved in a heated debate. The conversation really caught my attention when one woman said, "I want to know when black men will change and become more sensitive to black women!" A man at her table quickly responded, "I guess black men will be more sensitive to black women when you sisters learn how to treat us better. I'm tired of all you black women running us down."

The debate raged on about which gender was to blame for the troubles between black men and women. Neither camp was willing to back down. The woman standing near me in line turned to me and smiled, shaking her head. She asked, "When will we ever get this straightened out?"

Friction between black men and women was also evident at a conference on male-female relations I attended recently in Nashville, Tennessee. A small group of black men stopped short as they approached the meeting-room door and saw that the room was almost filled, mostly with black women. One man turned to another and said, "It looks like a lynching to me." Hesitant to lay themselves open for the blame and ridicule they apparently thought was forthcoming, the men retreated. Their behavior made me think of the movie *Jungle Fever*, in which Spike Lee and Wesley Snipes cower outside Snipes's home while his wife and her friends meet inside in what Lee describes as a "war council." I find it sad that many black men expect a roomful of sisters to be enemy territory.

While a number of black men and women enjoy good loving, many others are trapped in a cycle of bitter emotions and disappointments. As I travel across the country conducting seminars and workshops on male-female relationships for African-American men and women, I am constantly bombarded by frustrated individuals struggling, often in silence, to find the love they want and feel entitled to. They talk in detail about the hostile nature of their relations. Many desperately seek a way to end the conflicts. They want answers from me. What has gone wrong between black men and women? Why can't they get along?

I hear the same questions from listeners who call in to my weekly radio talk show, *All About Love*, on WHUR-FM, in Washington, D.C. I have been on the air for over ten years, yet my callers continue to express growing impatience with the battle between the sexes. And those who think that only women are interested in relationship issues are wrong; hundreds of black men call in to my radio show and attend my seminars for tips on how they might love black women better—and be loved and accepted in return. Among the undergraduate and graduate students I counsel at Howard University, the same concerns surface.

The struggles of black men and women with their love relationships are also the focus of my private practice in the Washington, D.C., area. Virtually all of my clients—whether single, married, or cohabiting—are looking for ways to build healthy relationships and avoid the all-too-familiar traps. My clients include African-American couples, interracial couples, international couples, gay and lesbian couples, and couples from diverse religious backgrounds. Some are doctors or lawyers, teachers or administrators, or struggling entrepreneurs. Others are first-generation college graduates, while a few have only a high school diploma and have worked many years to obtain a level of economic success.

And I cannot go to a social gathering without the topic of black male-female relationships coming up. At one party recently I met a man who was clearly anxious because he was there alone. As we talked, his eyes darted around the room, no doubt looking to see how many of us were coupled off. When he found out what I did for a living, he followed me around all night long, badgering me with questions about why he and the rest of "the brothers" couldn't find a good woman. When I told him to relax, he insisted that he had to have an answer because he couldn't go on any longer by himself.

Like so many of my clients and radio listeners, this man was eager to find support among others who feel frustrated and disappointed about their romantic possibilities. When people are hurting emotionally, they want to know that they are not alone, that others are grappling with similar issues. I can relate to this feeling because I have been there myself.

I married when I was far too young to understand the many nuances of a relationship. I naïvely believed that if I did everything right—that is, everything my husband expected of me—then all would be well. My marriage gave me a desired role in life, a reason for being, and for many years this was more than enough for me. Yet I realized after almost ten years that my husband and I were not talking as we had at first, and he seemed less and less satisfied with my efforts to please him. When I allowed myself to focus on the many silent places in our marriage, I became frightened. Arguing between mates I could understand; dead silence was new to me.

It was during a wedding anniversary celebration that I finally got up enough nerve to ask my husband why we didn't talk anymore. Much to my surprise, he seemed eager to respond. He launched into a monologue about black women and how difficult it can be to understand them. "Some women know how to be good to a man, nurture him, and be sensitive," he said. After a while it was evident that he was talking, not about women in general, but about a very specific woman. And I knew he wasn't talking about me.

I felt sad, scared, and helpless. A friend suggested that I join her at a weekend spiritual forum where people talked about setting goals for improvement in their lives. During that weekend I realized that the search for answers is an ongoing part of the human condition, and that asking for help is not a sign of weakness. I was ultimately unsuccessful in my attempts to save my marriage, but I can trace back to that time the beginning of my interest in relationships and of my determination to discover why they are such a puzzle to so many.

A Boy—And a Beginning

An experience with a four-year-old boy and attendance at a training conference for teachers first got me interested in family systems theory.

Before receiving my training as a therapist, I was a preschool teacher and director in New Haven, Connecticut. It was then that I realized the direct relationship between children's home environments and how children act—or act out—in school. One boy, Adam, particularly brought this point home. Although preschool staff are not supposed to have favorites, we all agreed that Adam was a particularly appealing child. A bright, articulate boy, Adam mastered skills early and always volunteered to be the teacher's helper. Perhaps because he was the only child of highly articulate and well-educated parents, Adam was very comfortable around adults, and even sought them out. I was director of the preschool then, and Adam always made a point of coming to my office each day with a cheery hello and a hug. Sometimes he brought me gifts—a special drawing or a pretty leaf he'd found on the sidewalk.

And then Adam's behavior began to change. He became sullen and difficult, and would whine or fight with little or no provocation. One day another boy took a toy from him, and Adam launched into a tantrum that stunned the children and teachers alike. He thrashed about on the floor, throwing books and toys around the room. And then, inexplicably, he ran to the toy phone and tore it from the wall.

The teacher brought Adam to my office. I lifted him on to my lap and held him close, and Adam sobbed as if the world were coming to an end. Finally he looked up at me and out of the blue said, "Daddy hit Mommy, and he tore the phone out of the wall. If you tell him what I did, he's going to get me too."

Adam was so sad and frightened, I told him that I should talk with his mommy and daddy. Reluctantly, he agreed.

Adam's parents were more than willing to meet with me. When I described the incident at school, they were mortified. Adam's mother dropped her head. "We're kind of not getting along right now," she whispered. "We've been fighting a lot. But we thought Adam was asleep when this was going on. I had no idea he heard us."

Adam's father, a dignified man for whom this conversation was obviously distressing, added that part of the fight was about whom Adam would live with when they separated, and he wanted very much for his son to be with him. I explained to them that these issues were very difficult for a four-year-old to comprehend, and that we were going to have to find help for Adam during this turbulent period in his parents' lives.

Since we were near Yale University, the most likely source of help for Adam was Dr. James Comer, a nationally recognized professor of child psychiatry and an associate dean at Yale, who at the time was with the Yale Child Study Center. Dr. Comer took on Adam's case and allowed me to maintain my involvement with the little boy and his family. I sat in on some of the meetings with them, and was able to see how closely interconnected family relationships are. Adam's parents were the two people he depended on most, and their disputes made him feel that the whole world was collapsing. His acting out at school was in part a reaction against their acrimony, but in part it stemmed from an unconscious desire to reunite his parents by giving them a common focus—their son's behavior. Dr. Comer had Adam use a family of small rubber dolls to act out what was happening with his family, then encouraged Adam to talk—to put words to his feelings. Adam became able to express how frightened and angry he felt about his parents' arguments.

The parents eventually divorced, but with Dr. Comer's help they were able to see that Adam would benefit most from joint custody. Adam continued to see Dr. Comer for a while to learn how to cope with his anger and frustration without acting out.

Not long after meeting Dr. Comer, I attended a conference on family systems theory conducted by Dr. Earl T. Braxton, a psychologist. I knew very little about psychotherapy; I was still a teacher and preschool director, and had not yet started my training as a counselor. Yet this conference, along with Adam's experience and the privilege of seeing Dr. Comer at work, set me on this path.

At the University of Bridgeport in Connecticut, I received a master's degree in counseling with a concentration in the study of family systems theory. And from there I proceeded to a doctoral program in clinical psychology and private practice. While most of my work today is with adults, I am often still guided by family systems theory. When I work with parents, I always have their little Adams (and Eves) in mind, for what the parents experience, their children live with, too.

External and Internal Struggles

Relationships do not exist in a vacuum. Historical, psychological, social, and cultural factors affect how men and women relate to one another. Both black men and black women tell me they feel misunderstood by a society that thwarts the attainment of their goals and aspirations while at the same time criticizing them for not doing any better. The injustice is compounded by the fact that many members of their own community stereotype and devalue them. Black women tell me they are tired of being expected to bear the burden for all the ills in the black community. Many seethe with anger that much is expected of them and rewards are few. On the other hand, black men often complain bitterly that society portrays them as endangered, dangerous, or just downright irresponsible.

African Americans who continue to face enormous economic and social disparities are also affected emotionally by their marginal status in this country. Couples may come to me fighting about money, intimacy, communication, and other typical relationship concerns. But invariably I find that the real struggles are internal, with one or both of the individuals feeling a lack of personal control, a sense of emotional deprivation, a need for nurturance, or a strong sense of helplessness.

In part, these struggles reflect the difficulties of living in a racist society, and in part they can be traced to the beginning—the family unit in which perceptions and attitudes about relationships first develop. We need to look at the ways boys and girls are socialized in the black community. Many children receive mixed messages about the true meanings of masculinity and femininity. The ways they learn to survive in our society may conflict with the skills needed to thrive in a relationship. The result is major tensions and misunderstandings that create a chasm between black men and women.

In this book we will look at the psychosocial dynamics that are the foundation of the struggle for power and equality in black relationships. While, of course, other ethnic groups also have such struggles, in this book I address issues specific to African Americans owing to their history, child-rearing practices, and societal pressures. I examine why unrealistic expectations and confusion about masculine and feminine roles are the two main reasons why black men and women continue to struggle with one another.

What this book will *not* do is sort through old data trying to make some assessment of who is to blame for the conflict. I was reluctant at first to report on any seeming dysfunction within the black family system because much has already been written about our struggles and pathologies. And yet we must face the truth about the imbalances that cause stress in our families because the continued marital disruptions and the rising number of single-parent homes won't move us closer to what we all need—good loving bonds that tie us together as one. When black men and women are polarized in their attempts to create loving connections, it is the children who pay the price. They need more healthy modeling of stable relationships between men and women.

Getting Started

Recently, as I was driving in my car and listening to music, I noticed an unusual percussive beat. I idly wondered why I'd never noticed that drum riff, since I had played the music tape many times before. When the tapping and knocking sounds continued through the next song, and became increasingly louder, I realized that it was no drum beat—it was my car! Subconsciously, I must have realized that the sound was "something wrong," but I ignored the problem until I could deny it no longer. I quickly turned into the nearest gas station, and discovered that if I'd kept on driving, my car might soon have been incapable of making any sound at all.

Denying the nagging presence of "something wrong" is a common experience for my black clients. Often, they stretch out the denial phrase so long that by the time they see me they are truly in crisis. One reason they put off seeking help is that black people approach so many personal issues with a sense of shame that it can be difficult to touch on sensitive issues without causing embarrassment or anger. It is likely that this book will cause both because there is no point in broaching a subject only to skirt around certain topics and totally avoid others. My clients say they appreciate the fact that no subject is off-limits in my office.

A friend of mine likes to say that real power in this life is learning "to play the hand that's dealt you." That's essentially what we do in this book: take a look at the hand that has been dealt African-American men and women and figure out how to reorder the deck so that both sides can be winners.

Loving is lak de sea. It's a "moving" thing, but still and all, it takes its shape from de shore it meets, and it's different with every shore.

—Zora Neale Hurston,
Their Eyes Were Watching God

1

The Way I See It

Do not depend on anyone else for your happiness. Happiness
is something a person acquires for themselves with their energy and the tools of their mind.

—J. CALIFORNIA COOPER,
In Search of Satisfaction

Charlene and Michael seemed the perfect couple to all who met them.
Each had been married briefly before, but had remained single many
years before remarrying. When they met each other, there was so much
to talk about. It was as though they had known each other for many years.
They soon discovered that being together and sharing was much more
fun than the single lives they had been leading.

Michael often joked that he felt as if he had been a bachelor all of his
life. Women, he said, were all over him once he divorced and he admitted
that the attention was fun. Shy by nature, he used to envy the guys in
college who seemed to collect the ladies the way some athletes collected
trophies. He got the chance to feel the same exhilaration of the chase after
his marriage broke up, and vowed to his friends that he would never
marry again.

"I was definitely not looking for a wife," Michael told me. "Wives
seemed like headaches to me. I saw the guys scheming on their ladies and
trying to figure how they could get some time to themselves, and I felt a
little lucky that the only person I reported to was me. Black women
always scared me a little. I adored my mother, but she could make the

whole house quake when she was mad and that image just stuck with me."

Charlene, on the other hand, had immersed herself in her career and raising her two children after her divorce. She dated occasionally, but found the men she was meeting to be shallow and basically "unserious." She had little time for anyone who didn't understand that her responsibilities to family came first. With a wave of the hand, she dismissed the idea of ever marrying again. She felt that black men were afraid of her, and she was tired of the games that resulted from this fear.

"It used to amaze me that my girlfriends could spend their weekends at clubs and parties looking for these guys who really didn't have all that much going for them," she told me. "You know the ones. They come on strong with the phony business cards and smooth lines, trying to make you believe how important they are. What they really want is to bed you down for the night. I know black guys who would hock their souls to lease a Jaguar or Benz just as a ticket to pull in the ladies. I hate all those games."

As Michael approached his fortieth birthday, he too started tiring of the dating games. He was surprised at the thoughts that overwhelmed him at times when he was home alone listening to music. After growing up in a close-knit family, something about his state didn't feel right. Charlene was not quite forty when they met, but close enough that she too was consumed by the "what-to-do-with-the-rest-of-my-life" questions. Even though Charlene's friends teased her about being jaded about marriage, it was clear to all who knew her that she was lonely for male companionship.

Mutual friends decided that Michael and Charlene should meet. A dinner party was carefully planned where they could come together, without any obligations to go any further if things didn't click. To no one's surprise, they took to each other like old friends meeting after a long separation. They were soon spending endless hours on the phone and were always rearranging their schedules to meet as often as possible. Within six months, the subject of marriage came up. After endless discussions about where to live, what to do about the children, and the other necessary details of combining two lives, a wedding date was set and everyone was thrilled for them.

Buoyed by the newfound stability of her home life, Charlene threw herself into her career as a management consultant, assuming that Michael would understand. He was less career-focused than she, but seemed much more organized on the home front. This seemed like a perfect balance to her, so she began to leave much of the running of the household to Michael while she worked long hours both in the office and at home. About six months into the marriage, she was promoted at the consulting firm where she worked and was thrilled with this recognition of her hard work.

While Charlene was whirling from one meeting to another, Michael began sensing that his own job was less than secure. The real estate industry was reeling from the grip of the recession, but he had been with his company many years and had always felt that he could stay there as long as he wanted. When the rumors of layoffs started, he became anxious, but didn't share his nervousness with Charlene, for whom all was going so well. He thought perhaps he could find another job. Then she would never need to know about his worries.

Finding another job proved as difficult as holding on to his current one. Michael's entire department was abolished and within twenty-four hours he was home without any solid job leads. What seemed even worse to him was the prospect of telling Charlene that he had been laid off. Much to his surprise, she was very supportive and reassured him that another job would turn up sooner than he imagined. She urged him to spend all his energy on his job search while she took care of everything else.

Weeks turned into months and no job materialized for Michael. He hated looking for work and saw every turndown as a personal rejection. To escape the doldrums, he started hitting the basketball courts every day and showing up at the popular happy-hour bars around town. Charlene eventually lost her patience and started giving him "to-do" lists each morning that he said made him feel like a child. Michael hated having her tell him how to look for a job, and adamantly refused her offer to redesign his résumé. She even arranged a job interview for him with a client, only to blow up in anger when she heard that he was thirty minutes late for the appointment.

The fighting escalated until Michael charged Charlene with "attacking his manhood." This really did it for Charlene; she had no patience with what she called "the black man's lament." Michael's statement caused her to launch into a litany of everything she had ever done to help him. She told me that she was genuinely baffled by his actions because she thought he was as ambitious as she. Michael was an articulate, well-educated guy, so Charlene couldn't figure out why he was so threatened by everything she tried to do.

The final break came when Charlene discovered that Michael was having an affair with an old girlfriend. He said that his old friend made him feel good about himself, and didn't beat up on him about his failures. He loved Charlene, but felt overwhelmed by what he saw as her need to control him. On the other hand, Charlene felt deeply betrayed by the man she had let down her guard to trust. She thought she was getting a partner, not another dependent. "You see," she told me, "no matter what you do for them it always ends up the same way." The "them" she was talking about were black men, and she vowed for all who would listen: "Never again."

Unfortunately, Charlene and Michael's story is not an unusual one. Similar tales of hostility and blame are played out in my office every day. Black women are called "Sapphires" after the forceful character on the old *Amos and Andy* radio and television shows, and described as controlling, castrating shrews. Black men are told they are unreliable, irresponsible cads, loving and leaving women who make great sacrifices for them. Black women talk about being the backbone of society and being tired of it. Black men, feeling powerless and insecure in a hostile world, complain about being misunderstood and under attack by almost everyone, especially their own women. Black women respond that black men are whiners and complainers and have it no harder in this world than they do. And so it goes, on and on.

That black men and women in this country are at war with each other is without question. The battles have gone on for years, but few have been willing to discuss them. Only now, with the statistics on the breakdown of the black family too awesome to ignore, are some experts willing to discuss a once forbidden topic. In 1970 more than 68 percent of all black families were headed by couples; today the figure has fallen to 44 percent. (The percentage dropped from 73 to 64 percent for whites during the same period.) The divorce rate for black couples has tripled in the same time period from 100 per thousand married persons to more than 300 per thousand, and the percentage of married adult black women has fallen from 70 percent in 1960 to 35 percent today.

A 1992 issue of *Black Enterprise* magazine reported a shocking statistic concerning the prospect of marriage for young black couples. An article on the plight of black men stated that "for black males under the age of 25, marriage is virtually nonexistent." A 1994 study in the *Journal of Marriage and the Family* cited a similar finding: 23 percent of all single black men—nearly one in four—said they intended never to marry, while only 13 percent of the black women and white men surveyed made a similar statement. Sociologist Scott South, who conducted the research, said that black men felt that the possibility of numerous alternatives made "it unnecessary for them to commit to one woman in order to attain the sexual and emotional advantages of marriage." The reality that an increasing number of black men are becoming less desirous of marriage offers little comfort to black women looking for suitable partners. In some age groups, the number of never-married black women is twice that of white women. And while much has been written about the breakdown of the American family in general, these statistics speak clearly to the fact that the black American family is in serious trouble.

Time was, that the only way to get a good dialogue going about relationships in the black community was for some author to publish a book lambasting black men or for some movie or theatrical production to come out depicting black men and women in stereotypical roles. I remember the furor when Michele Wallace's book *Black Macho and the Myth of the Superwoman* was published, when the movie based on Alice Walker's novel *The Color Purple* hit the movie theaters, and when Ntozake Shange's play *for colored girls who have considered suicide / when the rainbow is enuf* opened. Many black men and even some black women castigated these writers as traitors to the cause of black people.

Wallace described herself as a black feminist writing about the chasm between black men and women—a subject that had been taboo up to that point. She criticized the black men of the civil rights movement for using the skills of black women to further their political goals while neglecting the women's own emotional and social needs. Wallace also asserted that the liaisons of black men and white women relegated black women to a backup role. These subjects had long been whispered about in the black community, but here Wallace was exposing them for the whole world to hear.

The Color Purple and *for colored girls* made legions of black men crazy with anger. They felt that the negative portrayal of black men in both works—as the abusive, wife-beating character "Mister" in Walker's movie, and as the many "ne'er-do-wells" in Shange's play—would cause the entire society to label all black men as rapists and wife-beaters. That both books were written by black women made some black men feel especially betrayed.

I went to see *The Color Purple* with a girlfriend because so many black men were up in arms about the film that I didn't dare ask a male friend to accompany me. But I saw *for colored girls* with a male colleague who admitted that he hoped viewing the play would be a cathartic experience, a way to rid himself of guilt about how he had mistreated some of the black women in his life. With this play, many black men were vividly confronted for the first time in their lives with the black female's viewpoint about her treatment at the hands of black men. I think black men who saw the play had such visceral reactions because their portrayal seemed so starkly one-sided. I'm sure many wondered who would speak up for them. For black women, the play offered a chance to share the pain they had been hiding for so many years. In this brief portion of one of my favorite monologues from the play, *lady in blue* captures what I feel is the experience of so many black women I know.

> one thing i dont need
> is any more apologies
> i got sorry greetin me at my front door
> you can keep yrs
> i dont know what to do wit em
> they dont open doors
> or bring the sun back
> they dont make me happy
> or get a mornin paper
> didnt nobody stop usin my tears to wash cars
> cuz a sorry
> i am simply tired

While this play was indeed harsh in its depiction of black men, it was a significant milestone for many black women who finally felt they had found a voice.

Terry McMillan's widely acclaimed novel *Waiting to Exhale*, published in 1992, is a witty and sometimes acerbic look at the attempts of four black women to find consistent loving from the men in their lives. Many black men and women used the book as a starting point for an honest discussion about relationship problems. I heard some black men complain about several of the "trifling" male characters in the book, but I heard even more say that it gave them insight into the real-life experiences of black women who are searching for love and marriage.

The root of the conflict for black men and women lies in an internalized sense of self-hatred that is absorbed from the broader society and then projected unwittingly onto one another. The bruised egos and unrealized aspirations that are part of growing up black in this society take a heavy toll emotionally. A psychiatrist friend told me that she believes that black people in this country live in a constant state of emotional distress. So instead of "the man" being the problem, black men and women become a problem for each other. For many black couples, it is just easier to fight each other than risk losing the larger battle of fighting what is perceived as a constricted and unfair world. Also, taking individual responsibility for what's wrong in a relationship seems more difficult to some of my clients than trying to get their partner to make changes.

Let's go back to Charlene and Michael, the couple we met in the beginning of this chapter. To all who saw them before he lost his job, their relationship seemed to be going well. He wanted to work and had done well on his job for many years. Finding work had never been a problem for him, but the 1991 recession had pushed many white-collar workers like Michael out of a job. Being jobless made him feel worthless, an emotion that is not uncommon after job loss. But Michael had heard all of his life about "not being a shiftless, lazy black man," and that being without a job meant that he was very much less than a man. He couldn't turn on CNN without hearing another story about black men who were in trouble, homeless, jailed, or embroiled in some other catastrophe. He hated these images of so-called endangered black men, and he couldn't stand the thought of being seen as a member of this group. Michael never articulated any of these emotions to his wife because this kind of intimate sharing seemed too unmanly to him. He shared his thoughts with me after weeks of counseling, but it took a great deal of probing. Many black men link talking about feelings with being too feminine and resist it at all costs. Opening up about a personal problem makes them feel dependent and exposed; they feel less than a man because they can't fix the problem themselves.

Charlene, on the other hand, was impatient with Michael's inability to talk about his troubles in finding a job. She wanted to see him assume responsibility for his situation and take appropriate and immediate action. She had grown up with a brother who at the age of thirty-two was still living at home with their parents. He came to her often with get-rich-quick schemes and other fly-by-night enterprises, and each time she saw her brother she wanted to scream. She was angry with her parents for "coddling him," and she admitted that she thought her brother was like most black men—running away from real responsibility. Her first husband was inconsistent with his child-support payments, often disappointed the kids when he promised to pick them up for an outing, and, to her way of thinking, was generally a "waste of time." Against this backdrop, it's easy to understand how she reacted when Michael looked like he was falling by the wayside. All she could think of was "Here I go again with another black man who is not going to make it."

Issues of blame regarding whose plight in life is worse are commonly bandied about by black couples in conflict, but rarely do they speak openly about what is the core of the problem. I might be able to show them how to solve some of the superficial issues that each claims to be distressed about, but the much larger underlying unrest remains. Since illumination is often the first step toward understanding any problem, let's look at what I see as the basic factors that keep black men and women struggling with paper tigers.

High Expectations and Disappointments

In both struggling and middle- to upper-class families, children are raised with high expectations that they will do well and make their family proud. Working-class parents want their children to reap greater rewards from society than they did. "Work hard and get an education," they urge, "and you'll make it." Yet for many, these goals of unprecedented social and economic success go unrealized, leaving them feeling unfulfilled and even cheated.

Black men and women from more affluent families are not only expected to succeed but also have high expectations about what life owes them. These individuals grew up with upwardly mobile parents who sheltered them from the harsh realities of racism by showering them with all the advantages money could buy. They led their children to believe that if they went to the right schools, joined the right organizations, and learned an appreciation for the finer things in life, everything else would come easily. Yet romantic relationships don't work that way. Instant gratification is the expectation, and relationships become disappointing when they cannot provide the enormous highs that some of these individuals have come to expect from life.

When expectations go unfulfilled, fantasy often steps in to fill the void. I see this often with the couples I work with. It's not uncommon for me to hear fantasies like that described by Savannah in McMillan's *Waiting to Exhale*:

Is it really possible to want something so bad that you could make it happen just by *thinking* about it? I mean, could I just dream myself up a husband? Wouldn't it sort of be like praying? A long time ago, I asked God to please send me a decent man, and one by one, what I got was Robert, Cedric, Raymond, and Kenneth. Unfortunately, I left out some very important details: Like how about a little compassion, some pride as opposed to cockiness, some confidence as opposed to arrogance. Now I'm more specific: Could You make sure he talks about what he feels and not just about what he thinks? Could he have a genuine sense of his purpose in life, a sense of humor, and could he already *be* what he aspired to? Could he be honest, responsible, mature, drug-free, and a little bit spontaneous? Could he be full of zest, good-enough-looking for me, and please let him be a slow, tender, passionate lover? It takes me forever to say my prayers these days, but I don't care, because this time around, I want to make sure God doesn't have to do any guesswork.

When black women describe some of their fantasies to me, they almost always include the perfect man who will make their life complete. Not only is he kind, handsome, loving, and supportive, but he is also rich. He is able to fix things—both material and emotional—when they are broken. He is a wonderful lover who, no matter what else is going on in his life, is sensitive and very attentive in bed. A great protector from harm, he is also a soulmate without peer. Of course, we all know that a perfect man does not exist anywhere for anyone. The result: disappointment beyond belief.

Charlene often told me of her dreams and how deeply disappointed she was that "things just didn't turn out right for her." In spite of her professional success, she felt that two failed marriages meant that she was doing something wrong in spite of her efforts to be all she could be.

"When I was in college, I loved riding the bus through the most expensive neighborhoods in town," she said. "My grades were always great and all of my instructors praised my work. So I thought that one of those big beautiful houses, surrounded by sloping lawns and lush trees, would be mine one day simply because I was doing so well. It never occurred to me that it wouldn't automatically happen. And it never occurred to me that I would have to get it all for myself. I was supposed to marry the doctor or lawyer and only work when the spirit moved me. And now it seems that all I do is work, work, work. I am too tired to even care about the big house anymore."

For many black men, the ultimate fantasy is the best mother he can imagine. She is accommodating, a tireless listener, and an unquestioning cheerleader. No matter what his shortcomings, she will be there to nestle his weary head on her bosom. What he wants is unconditional love, but romantic love always comes with conditions. The result: profound disappointment again.

Michael talked at length in the session about his mother. It was clear that she had provided much of his emotional sustenance all of his life. When things started unraveling with Charlene, he thought of his mother first. What would she say? What would she tell him to do? He told me that Charlene even looked like his mother and had many of the same mannerisms, but she wasn't as patient. Charlene talked fast and made him nervous.

"I couldn't seem to think fast enough or move fast enough for her,"

Michael said. "Sometimes after a day looking for work, I didn't want to talk or sort out any issues. I wanted her to understand what it was like going from one job interview to another. I wanted her to wait until I could talk about my feelings. But whatever I did wasn't enough. All she ever talked about was money and getting ahead, which is okay, but not when I didn't have any prospects of a job. My mother seemed to know instinctively what was happening with me. I wanted Charlene to be the same way."

Loving partnerships are built on reality. Fantasies may never come to fruition. In the meantime, life and potential (though less-than-perfect) partners pass some people by. Until we are willing to let go of unrealistic fantasies, black men and women cannot face each other as loving equals. What I find sad is the sheer numbers of men and women who spend many years of their adult lives looking for these fantasy partners, experiencing one disappointment after another. By the time they end up in my office, their condition borders on hysteria. Breathlessly, they tell me that they have tried everything and nothing seems to work. They still feel alone and deeply disappointed.

The Devil Is in the Numbers

The widespread belief that black men are relatively scarce worries—even panics—many black women. It is a fact that the black community is losing its men in ever-increasing numbers to joblessness, drug wars, homicide, and incarceration. Increasingly, men aren't around to help build marriages or raise children, primarily because of educational and economic inequalities. The Reverend Jesse Jackson has made famous the saying that there are more black men in prison than in all the colleges and universities in the United States. It is difficult to commit to a family when you don't have sufficient resources to create stability for yourself.

The endless media reports about the numbers of black women who will live their lives alone because of the shrinking pool of marriageable black men makes it easy to understand why so many women are obsessed with finding and keeping a man, no matter what the quality of the relationship. Black men know well that many women have become desperate. As a consequence some become arrogant and cocky in their "favored status," deciding that they can pretty much have their own way with any woman they meet.

When my clients relate stories about inferior dating and marital situations they are settling for, it is clear that they have become victims of the numbers game. When I ask why a client is staying in a relationship that is obviously causing a great deal of unhappiness, I get answers like these: "If I don't do this for him, when and where will I find another man? Is it fair for me to be alone?" And a line I hear frequently from men is: "What is she going to do about it; where is she going to find another guy like me?"

One forty-year-old man told me, "I give them what they want. I am a single black man who is well educated, well traveled, and I have plenty of money to spend. Most black women see me as a good catch, which means I get to call the shots most of the time. I have a woman who comes to see me from New York about once a month and I make sure she has a good time. Then there is another one I see when I travel to L.A. on business, and there is my steady in Oakland where I live. I know it sounds cocky, but they are glad to see me whenever I can work it out. Each must know that I see other women, but that doesn't change anything."

The number of available black men is not likely to change in the near future. The ratio is not going to be in black women's favor for many years to come. Clearly, though, the answer is not to put up with unacceptable behavior merely to keep a man. Some black women find creative solutions. They date men of other ethnic groups and cultures, or decide to go it alone, or see several men and accept that these men also see other women, or see one man and do not demand that he be monogamous.

It is this last choice that I discussed in my first book, *Man Sharing: Dilemma or Choice?* I was widely accused of promoting the notion that black women should accept sharing their men sexually and emotionally with other women since there were so few good available black men. In several books by other writers I am "credited" with introducing this radical idea. Just recently at a reception, I was chatting with a small group of women when another joined the group. When introduced to me, she immediately said, "Oh yeah, I know her. She's that woman who was trying to make black women do something they will never do."

The media hype about *Man Sharing* caused many to believe that I was truly advocating polygamy as a reasonable way of life. Rather, I was only urging women to realistically confront a troubling social condition and consider *all* of the alternatives. I also wanted to shed some light on the explosive issue of affairs and help women learn to cope better with their depression and sense of helplessness about this painful dilemma.

The heated reaction to my book surprised me. Strange things began to occur. Black women attacked me, and black men began to look at me with a gleam in their eye because they thought I was sanctioning having more than one woman at a time. To set the record straight: I *never* condone sexual exploitation. I *do* favor giving women more choices and empowering them to set their own course.

Black women sometimes throw me a curve ball. At workshops and in therapy sessions they lament, "Why won't he commit to me and me alone?" Then they go on the offensive when I impart the bad news: many men still prefer more than one woman at a time, and this fact isn't likely to change however much women deny it.

I think what black women are really angry about is the loss of their fantasies. One black single woman in a workshop said angrily, "How dare you tell us that we might not find a man? I have done everything I was supposed to do. I have a good education, a great job, I own my own home, and I have traveled all over the world. Now I want to settle down and have a family, and you're saying it might not happen for me and I resent it." Some of the married women who attend my relationship workshops insist that their partners will never step out on them with another woman—as if denying this possibility loudly enough can keep it from happening.

It is painful but true that the man shortage means that many black women will not find partners to have just for themselves. Yet women need not be victims. In *Man Sharing* I discussed the type of attitude necessary for a woman to survive a partner's affair, and described women who had this attitude as "Women of Choice." They set the rules for their own behavior and leave relationships that don't offer fulfillment. They refuse to permit men to use affairs as a tool to whip women into shape and avoid commitment. Too many of my female clients cry to me about what they are willing to do to keep a man away from other women, even if it means changing who they are. This is a hopeless game that keeps too many women trapped in unsatisfying relationships. My ultimate advice is always the same: learn to love and take care of yourself.

The Great Divide—Economics and Education

Part of the numbers game for black women is the whole notion of selection—whom they choose and why. Black women are often criticized for their emphasis on the superficial. Black men often feel that if they don't have the requisite material wealth, women will regard their internal qualities as inconsequential. The trouble is that many black women feel that they deserve and are entitled to an idealized mate—a romantic partner who is also a "man of means." Black men know this, and some concoct games of pretend in order to lure the woman with dollar signs in her eyes. For example, a man might carry phony credentials like a gold-embossed card with a company name listing him as the president of the firm. Or he might lease a car he can ill afford. The relationship thus begins with an assumption and a lie: an assumption that the woman seeks riches, and a lie that a man has them.

There are many who would say that there is only one reason black men and women can't get along—economics. It is no secret that black men have a difficult time in the marketplace. According to researcher Delores P. Aldridge in the work *Black Male-Female Relationships: A Resource Book of Selected Materials*: "In the last decade and a half, the median income of black males never reached two-thirds of the median income of white males. Perhaps even more striking is the fact that the income gap has repeatedly shown signs of widening. Although black females appear to compare more favorably with white females than black males with white males, in reality, they fare worse than either one of the other groups."

Some black men are angry because they believe black women have succeeded during the seventies and eighties at their expense. Statistics don't support their belief, but it persists just the same. The truth is that two out of three black children are born to unmarried women, meaning that black women are struggling economically to raise children by themselves. And in terms of a paycheck, black women are *last* on the list—behind white men, white women, and black men. In 1992 the median income was $8,816 for black women and $12,962 for black men. Yet the myth persists that black women are doing well at the expense of black men.

One reason the myth endures is the high visibility of some black women who in recent years have risen through the corporate ranks. In 1994 the *Wall Street Journal* reported that black women professionals in corporate America outnumbered black men two-to-one. The article also noted that the ranks of professional black women grew 125 percent between 1982 and 1992 among companies reporting figures to the U.S. Equal Employment Opportunity Commission. The problem with such reports is that they fuel the debate between black men and women about who is doing better economically. Furthermore, it is grossly unfair to focus on the small group of women who have climbed the corporate ladder when huge numbers of black women are continuing to struggle.

In higher education, black women accounted for about 6 percent of people aged seventeen to thirty-four who were enrolled in institutions of higher learning in 1988. The figure for black men was only 4.5 percent. From 1990 to 1991, African Americans recorded a 7.1 percent gain in total enrollment in higher education. African-American women experienced a slight decline from 1990 to 1991 in the participation rates of high school graduates in college. Nonetheless, the 1991 rate of 30.9 percent reflects a 6 percent gain overall for African-American women since 1985.

During the 1980s, African-American female graduates showed more progress in higher-education participation than African-American male graduates. Yet thus far, the 1990s show a slight reversal in this trend. In 1991, 32.2 percent of African-American male high school graduates enrolled in college, compared with the 30.9 percent figure for females.

But despite obvious gains, power and the perquisites of the good life are not available to the majority of black men, and they are painfully aware of this fact. Does this lowered economic status affect how a black man deals romantically with a black woman? Remember the old adage that there's no romance without finance. This seems to be especially true in the black community. A black male college student told me that he worries about his ability to attract a "superstar sister." Without a lot of money or the appearance of some money, he believes his chances with most black women are slim.

Another young man, Jason, a thirty-year-old electrician who is working to complete a college degree, told me, "The sisters only want brothers who are together with a career. They won't even go out with us if we don't have a car. They want us to be making millions or they won't even talk to us. They say we are not up to par if we don't look prosperous." So unequal educational levels and imbalanced economics play a direct role in the power dynamics that go on between black men and women, eroding the passion they both long for and deserve.

Racism or Sexism—Which Is Worse?

If one clear issue was brought out during the Clarence Thomas–Anita Hill sexual harassment hearings on Capitol Hill, it was that black people are divided about what is more important to fight—racism or sexism. Hill, who testified that Supreme Court nominee Thomas had sexually harassed her for a number of years while she worked for him, was criticized bitterly among many blacks for "turning in a brother." Black women were enraged at Anita Hill just as they were at Desiree Washington for accusing boxer Mike Tyson of raping her. These two women were vilified in the black community for openly discussing what many consider a taboo subject. Women are not supposed to talk about the way some black men treat them. Those who do are often shunned, not only by black men but by their sisters as well. Black women are expected to protect black men, harassment or no harassment.

Hill and Washington were seen as traitors, as willing collaborators with a white society that often seems intent on bringing black men down. I heard black women call Hill and Washington liars, pawns, and conniving manipulators who were only out to help themselves. Some black women's harshest remarks were reserved for Washington, who was widely criticized for even being in a hotel room with Tyson. Many claimed that she set him up and then cried to the world about what he had done to her. Both cases are examples of how some black women collude in the chauvinistic behavior of some black men because they do not want to identify with their own oppression.

I believe that the sexist mindset of many black men has been one of the best-kept secrets in the black community. Younger black men have become more open about it; some rappers even flaunt blatant sexism in their lyrics. I am surprised that more black women are not up in arms about being called "hoes" and "bitches" in so many black films and songs. I would like to see more protests like that held by the Congress of Black Political Women in Washington, D.C. They called for an end to the negative attitudes about black women so often a part of "gangsta rap" and threatened a national boycott of record stores that sold records with degrading lyrics.

I cannot remember a time when black male filmmakers and musicians have made more ugly references to the black woman's temperament, her anatomy, her physical appearance, and her behavior. I came of age listening to the Motown sound, whose love songs celebrated black women's beauty and grace. I loved Smokey Robinson's songs because my friends and I could all imagine that he was singing to us. What self-respecting black woman can get turned on by lyrics like "I like the crotch on you" and by rappers' references to "doing her"?

Music videos should offend enough black women to start a massive national boycott, yet there is only a deafening silence from many young black women. When I suggest to some of my college-age clients that they should be appalled by their depiction in such videos, they have not the slightest notion why I am so bothered. It offends me to see black womanhood celebrated on the screen as scantily clad "hot mommas" rolling around on silk sheets, but I hear few complaints from black women about how these depictions marginalize them into solely sexual beings. Black men have gotten away with their sexist behavior because they have successfully kept our focus on racism.

A young writer, Kevin Powell, described his own struggle with racism and sexism in a 1992 article in *Essence* magazine:

> I recalled my childhood. I evolved as many boys do in this society: Machoism gripped my psyche, and by the time I reached my teen years we "boys" did whatever we felt like doing—which ran the gamut from squeezing girls' buttocks in gym class to "gangbanging" girls in abandoned buildings. Even after my political consciousness blossomed in college, I self-righteously continued to rationalize that the real battle was against racism, and if the sistas on campus couldn't fall into line, well, then, those women weren't really down with the program anyway.

To some extent, black men and women perpetuate the existence of sexism, however, by denying their roles in its persistence in the community. Young black men are not encouraged by older black men to take ownership of sexist attitudes and behaviors. Instead, the young men feel entitled to these attitudes: they are a means of keeping the upper hand with their women. Because many black men feel so dominated and powerless about their ability to negotiate with the women in their lives (sisters, aunts, grandmothers), they resort to sexist attitudes in order to gain some semblance of control.

Most black men do not want to consciously acknowledge this fact, but many admit to it during private moments. In large male groupings they joke about how they control women by perpetuating the double standard. A man in one of my group sessions said, "You got to keep them dependent upon you for certain experiences. Just when she seems too self-assured about the relationship, I become distant with her so she'll panic about her status and behave more docilely instead of aggressive and controlling. You got to find a way to keep black women in their place."

Black women learn early in their social development to deny the sexism to which they are subjected. They are in an unusual predicament. Often, by the time a black girl reaches adolescence, the expectation that relationships with black men will be harsh, oppressive, and intense has been ingrained in her mind. The black women I see have a subconscious attitude that I call "internalized oppression," an almost tacit acceptance that they as women will be mistreated by both society and black men. Although many of these women have witnessed sexist behavior throughout their development, they have no real language to express or label this type of oppression. It is just something that happens.

In her book *Deals with the Devil*, Atlanta author Pearl Cleage says:

> It is impossible to live in America and not be tainted by sexism and a participant in it, either as a victim or a perpetrator. As women, by the end of our African-American girlhoods, we have learned and perfected a dizzying variety of slave behaviors which are rewarded for mastering by the men who made them

up in the first place. Sexism (and racism) are systems of oppression designed to control, confine and exploit one group of people for the benefit of another group of people. In discussions of sexism, black women are the oppressed and black men are the oppressors.

For various reasons, even in the 1990s, many black women are still confused about their responsibility for ending sexist thinking within the black community. In the 1982 underground bestseller, *The Blackman's Guide to Understanding the Blackwoman*, Shahrazad Ali suggested that black women created their own problems by not playing their roles correctly with black men. Ali felt that black women owed it to black men to be subservient and quietly accepting of their men's sexist behavior. Ali's unrealistic, oppressive assumption only reinforced black men's sexist attitudes and black women's guilt.

Black women must speak out widely about sexism, not just discuss it among themselves. Even when harassed on the job, raped by a date, or beaten by a lover, many suffer in silence. They won't risk public censure by complaining about their treatment at the hands of a black man. As many have learned, taking on a brother in public virtually assures a black woman of the ridicule and hostility of her community. The distorted thinking goes something like this: "After all, if black men are in such peril, how can you blame them or hold them responsible for lapses in appropriate behavior?" Or "My goodness, they have enough stresses in their life—we sisters need to be behind our men no matter what."

Redefining Gender: The Search for Self

While there is no denying that unfulfilled expectations, economic and educational disparities, the scarcity of available black men, and battles over racism and sexism shape much of the tension I see between black men and women, the underlying reason the battle persists has more to do with each gender's search for a clear definition and acceptance of self. Finding a constructive definition of masculinity and femininity is a difficult process for many of my clients.

Many of the men and women I counsel feel they have been searching much of their lives for a missing part of their identity. They are trying to compensate, through romantic attachments, for lost emotional experiences from childhood. This is often a fruitless journey, an unrealistic expectation of a partner.

I believe that most black girls and boys grow up with a confused sense of gender identity, thus making adult romantic connections a game of chance at best. By gender identity I do not mean what usually passes for the man's role or the woman's role, as in who washes the dishes and who mows the lawn. Rather, I speak of the essential feminine and masculine traits that are intrinsic parts of every person's character. Psychologists define feminine traits as the soft side of one's nature: being nurturing, dependent, nonassertive. Masculine traits include being independent, distant, aggressive, and domineering. For optimum mental health, an individual needs a healthy integration of these masculine and feminine traits, or what I call *gender blending*.

In many black adults, gender roles are confused or seriously out of balance because of the manner in which children are raised. Girls are likely to get tremendous support in the development of their masculine side—which reinforces feelings of independence, self-reliance, and the need to dominate or control the outcome of one's life—at the expense of the soft or feminine side. At the same time, black boys often get only a part of their masculine side developed, and they learn to mistrust any display of the feminine. A young black boy's dependence on women creates for him an overdeveloped sense of masculinity—or *machismo*—as a protection from being what some would call "sissified."

Society provides few economic or social props to support the growth of healthy black families, so too many black children grow into adulthood seeking the balance and harmony in romantic relationships that they find lacking in their families and community. This aimless search for romantic liaisons that will serve as a panacea for all life's ills and inequalities brings about fractured relationships between the sexes. What ensues are bitter battles between black men and women, with each party trying to get from the other what is needed to make him or her feel whole. Couples coming in for counseling may present obvious signs of this gender imbalance, but rarely does either party recognize this as their real problem. (I discuss this issue in more depth in chapter 3.)

Charlene and Michael's situation is illustrative of how black couples struggle with gender-role influence. When Michael lost his job and Charlene got her promotion, he experienced the role reversal as an attack on his manhood and felt she was out to make him into a dependent, dominated spouse. Because he had never fully separated from his mother, he was uncertain about his masculine identity. Not having a father around to support the developmental process of gender identity caused Michael to struggle in silence with issues concerning authority and masculinity. Ultimately, Michael's confused feelings about gender roles impaired his ability to cope with his vulnerability within a romantic relationship.

Charlene struggled in her own way. She knew that Michael faced a racist workplace every time he sought employment, but since she had survived, she thought that he should, too. She didn't want to hear about how "the man" was keeping black men down because she had to deal with "the man" herself. Instead of empathizing with Michael, Charlene did the only thing she knew how to do: take charge and rescue the family situation before there was tragedy.

How often have we heard a black man say: "She won't let me be a man"? Many black men truly believe that black women want to control them, and they will design absolutely silly games to avoid any perception that they are being dominated. A simple question like "What time will you be home?" can send a man into a defensive, hostile posture. One man at a black family conference once told me that no black woman was going to "control his penis." When I asked what he meant by this statement, he replied that he stays out all night at least once a month just to prove to his wife that she can't tell him what to do.

Black women play into the fears of black men by spending endless hours trying to gain access to their men's emotions, only to become enraged, depressed, and act out in revenge when their men fail to respond. Most black women have difficulty understanding that "opening up" is a frightening experience for the average black male. All of his social training tells him to deny his "soft side" in order to survive psychologically and socially. And she, too, has been told to mistrust her own "soft side." Her upbringing reinforces her masculine traits because the assumption is that she will need them in order to survive on her own.

When there is not enough differentiation between the masculine and feminine, or an inappropriate blending of the two traits, a breakdown occurs within the individual's emotional system. Boundaries become blurred. The man has to resist identifying with the feminine energy within the union, and the woman flees from her own feminine energy. Both black men and black women struggle with the same dynamic: owning their "feminine" energy and allowing the masculine to comfortably blend with it. The resulting gender imbalance is the very dynamic that sets the stage for the battle over entitlement and power between black men and women, a situation I explore in greater detail in chapter 2. In contrast, when gender blending does occur an individual feels less defensive or frightened of real intimacy.

Many of my male clients openly express their fears of getting too close to a black woman. She seems too demanding or overpowering, they often say, and this brings to mind the deep-seated fear of emasculation that haunts, to some degree, virtually every black man in America. They express their fear of women covertly by making hostile comments about women being cold and uncaring. These men often describe a castration fantasy in which black women strip them of their manhood by withholding love, affection, and sex. Most black men greatly fear the abandonment of the women they depend upon for love, nurturance, and affirmation, but they are just as frightened of getting too close.

These men say they need and love women, but they don't know how to give of themselves and protect their hearts at the same time. Men in general often experience this sense of vulnerability in making love connections, but for black men it is more significant because their women are perceived as omnipotent "Earth Mothers" who can turn a man into Jello with little more than a glance. This is how Michael perceived Charlene, and he defended against this feeling of vulnerability in every way he could.

Many black men and women grow up with a great void and need for emotional closeness, but are taught in hundreds of ways that they won't find this fulfillment in each other. Trust is nonexistent because each is too wary of the other to let go just a little emotionally. This was the case for Charlene and Michael, who decided the path to a healthy relationship was too difficult for them, so they eventually divorced. If only they had looked back, they could have seen that their conflict stemmed in part from their individual personal histories. The truth is that they had been set up by a variety of factors over which they had little control.

2

Raising Our Daughters, Loving Our Sons: The Setup

We are the children of those who chose to survive.

—NANA POUSSIANT, *Daughters of the Dust*

When Gena and Sam came in for counseling, they seemed like many young single couples I see who are grappling with a general sense of incompatibility that creeps in after several years of living together. She summed up her feelings this way: "I just can't talk to him. He doesn't listen." Sam said the only thing he wanted to talk about was why she never wanted sex anymore, and whether or not there was something wrong with him.

I explained to the couple that a vital part of the first session for all clients was my taking a family history, social history, and sexual history; without this information I'd have no road map to guide me. Pen and paper in hand, I began to ask questions, only to be stopped by both.

"Wait a minute. Why do you need to know about my parents, siblings, and relatives?" Gena said. "This is between Sam and me. My family has absolutely nothing to do with this."

"Yes, but you know how much you act like your mother," Sam offered. "You've said that yourself."

"Okay, okay, but what does that have to do with the problems we have now?" she said. "How long is it going to take to make us get along better?"

Many black couples I counsel resist going back to their childhood, even after I explain how critical the process is to unraveling their current problems. They seem to want a quick fix from me and less "prying." They want me to determine exactly what their problems are and tell them up front how many sessions it will take to solve them. The radio show I host presents a dilemma for my clients because they hear me give back answers to callers in a hurry, and they believe that a real therapy session can be handled just as quickly. However, I always caution my listeners that what I offer on the radio is just a quick, "on air" opinion and that therapy is a complex and time-consuming process.

Black men and women have no choice but to go back and unravel their pasts because buried within their family histories are the answers to the problems they are facing today. We can never escape our pasts. The slights, the hurts, the deprivations are always just beneath the surface, and these emotions get played out dramatically in personal relationships. Traditional couples therapy does not take into account the nontraditional way that many black boys and girls are socialized, and how this socialization affects their social-psychological development and how they relate to one another.

I believe that many in the black community employ a parenting style that ultimately pits males and females against one another. Families in which black girls are taught self-reliance and independence and black boys are pampered and protected are all too familiar in our communities. Many black boys are excused from what is considered "female work" and only girls are given any real household responsibilities. This style of relating to some black boys can reinforce an irresponsible attitude as they develop. For a variety of reasons, black women (and men) don't encourage their sons as often toward independence as they do their daughters. Sometimes the young male child is kept dependent so he'll stay close to a single mother and eventually play the role of the co-parent or "man of the house."

Part of black women's need to protect males is a reaction to the widespread belief that the world is a threatening place for black males. Indeed, mothers' terrors are real: police brutality, street violence, and drug wars claim all too many black men. No wonder black mothers strive to protect their sons. Their fears are not unlike those of slave women who worried that their sons would be lost at the hands of angry masters or rampaging Klansmen.

Ultimately, overprotecting sons by keeping them dependent does them a disservice. It deprives them of the ability to view themselves as independent, responsible people—and virtually guarantees that they will experience friction with their future mates. Even in homes where a man is present, the pervading belief in the black community that girls need to learn to take care of themselves, and that boys need to be protected from the ever-present racist evils "out there," causes parents to push their sons and daughters in different directions. These differing expectations for boys and girls give rise to adult men and women who are at one another's throats, unable to fulfill one another's romantic expectations. The result: a classic battle of the sexes, where the dynamics of entitlement, competition, resentment, and frustration are played out in the arena of love and passion. The style of parenting used to raise black boys and girls is a critical component of this ongoing power struggle. The "setup" begins before children leave the cradle, and the explosion takes place in adulthood.

The Hand That Rocks the Cradle

The adage that "the hand that rocks the cradle rules the world" certainly describes the current family experience in the black community. A staggering number of black mothers are rocking the cradles and running their households alone. Even in homes where a father is present, more often than not the mother is still seen as the dominant figure. This so-called matriarchal system has been blamed for much that is wrong in our communities, but it exists more out of necessity than by design.

Blaming the black woman for her strength is inherently unfair, but black men do it anyway. They blame the black woman for making black men feel inadequate. They require her to be a "superwoman," then fault her for being *too* strong. Less often do they acknowledge that the black woman lives a life of self-sacrifice, refraining from meeting her own physical or emotional needs until she addresses those of the people she must take care of.

I recall a friend of mine who was once in a car accident and suffered minor injuries. She was seen at the hospital and released, but insisted on taking a cab home instead of accepting a friend's offer to pick her up and take her home safely. My friend felt uncomfortable being "pampered" by anyone. She was so conditioned to be strong and independent that it did not occur to her that she could accept this offer without guilt and allow herself the joy of being taken care of for a change.

Parenting others is a common role for many black women who grow up seeing the women in their families derive their identity only through mothering roles. One woman complained to me that black women develop the mother role to the exclusion of all others. They see the role of mother as so pivotal that they come to believe that the whole black community sinks or swims based on how well they do this one job. Many black women are so invested in giving to and taking care of others that they lose all sense of what they need for themselves, not only as mothers but as women.

Changes in the black community's approach to child rearing are necessary if we are to unlock the conflict and tensions between black men and women. Dr. Jawanza Kunjufu, president of African-American Images, Inc., and a professor at Temple University, has called for a whole new structure of child rearing in the black community, so that we can nurture emotionally whole and healthy adults. He accuses black women of "raising their daughters and loving their sons," creating women who are self-sufficient and men who lack self-confidence and a sense of responsibility toward others. This dynamic also produces black men and women with entirely different views of what will be expected of them in adult relationships. The women learn that controlling their environment is a must if they are to take care of themselves and their families. And the men learn to fight this control with every means at their disposal.

Historically, black women have been forced to be the caretakers of the family because black men have not been able economically to play the role of breadwinner and father-protector. Black women have accepted this responsibility, but not without great resentment. They are in an untenable position: black women get praised or blamed for what happens with their children. If something goes wrong with a child, it is perceived that she didn't do her job well.

To discuss this issue of child rearing with a group of black women is tantamount to facing a firing squad. Black mothers tell me that they didn't ask to rear children alone and that they would welcome a willing male partner. "But where is he?" they want to know. They accuse me of blaming them—the real victims—when I ask for an honest assessment of their attitudes toward raising boys and girls. Black women alone cannot change the way boys and girls are reared; they need the involvement of men. To help both girls and boys develop healthy identities, a child's father—or a male family friend or social relation such as a minister— should be present to establish male bonding and modeling. It takes input from both genders to establish balanced roles that children can observe and internalize in their minds and emotions.

When the father role is diminished, many young boys and girls spend lifetimes searching for this missing experience. In his book *The Wounded Male*, Stephen Farmer emphasizes this point, saying that the ramifications of father absence during childhood are too great to be ignored:

> In order for a boy to establish his identity as a male, to learn what it means to be a man, he must give up his attachment to his first love—his mother. This in itself is a wound that a boy will have difficulty reconciling when his father is remote or altogether absent. If the father is not available to guide the boy away from mother, what results is an unfinished task of separation from mother and an incomplete relationship with a father figure. This leads to dependency on women, but one that is fraught with ambivalence.

For black boys, the longing for a father or some other consistent male mentor is ever present, even when their mothers are strong, dependable, and loving. Boys need constructive contact with other males to complete the process of healthy individuation and separation. Otherwise, they are left to the trial-and-error method of learning what a man is and does. Some black women minimize the need for men in their children's lives, but experience and research have shown me that black boys must have the input of good role models in order to develop healthy self-images of who they are. When young boys relate to parental adult males, they learn how to accept authority figures and identify with that same sense of power within themselves. This also helps them develop inner gender balance. Male bonding acknowledges them as young men and enables them to enter a romantic partnership later on without fearing loss of their sense of self. They can feel free to express both the male and female sides of their personalities without the nagging fear of seeming too soft, too feminine, or too tough.

One black mother of a grown son and daughter is now full of regret about how she reared her son. "I wish I had allowed his father a role, but I honestly didn't believe this man was capable of taking care of anybody. When they visited him they would come home with clothing messed up, shoes not polished, and so on. But now I know that these things didn't really matter. They did need their father."

This mother feels that her daughter is doing better than her son, who "had to struggle when he became nine or ten with what it meant to be a male. He began to question the right of the women in the family to define who he was and what was proper for a boy to do. We found out that he was urinating outside like some of the other boys, and I blew up. When I chastised him, he simply said that girls would do it too if it was as easy for them as boys. It was clear to me that he was questioning my rules and my standards of behavior for him as he found his way among his peers on the street. It's a cruel hoax for black women to feel they can be both parents. They cannot teach a boy about being a black man."

I don't believe our different approaches to raising boys and girls are always conscious. Practices develop over generations and they are all we know how to do. Mama is the lifeline in the black community, and her power has lifelong ramifications for both the male and female children growing up. With the absence of so many black fathers, there is no balance for either male or female children—no buffer. What results for both boys and girls is a skewed notion of how men and women can share power and display balanced gender roles without conflict.

Mothers and Sons

For a boy to develop as masculine in our culture, he must abandon the feminine style of the mother in favor of the more action-oriented, individualistic style of what this society defines as masculine. Unfortunately, in this process of individuation "fighting the feminine" becomes a way of life for too many black men.

A black boy learns early that black women are in control, and in many cases are to be feared. While a boy loves and depends upon his mother, she must also seem awesomely powerful. She decides what happens with him and how he should behave.

Ben Carson, M.D., a renowned black pediatric neurosurgeon, describes the breakup of his parents marriage in his autobiography, *Gifted Hands*. As in many black single-parent homes, his mother encompassed enough power for two parents, and exerted a strong influence over her sons' lives:

> Sonya Carson has the classic Type A personality—hardworking, goal-oriented, driven to demanding the best of herself in any situation, refusing to settle for less. She's highly intelligent, a woman who quickly grasps the overall significance rather than searching for details. . . . Because of that determined, perhaps compulsive personality that demanded so much from herself, she infused some of that spirit into me. . . . Mother had only a third-grade education when she married, yet she provided the driving force in our home. She pushed my laid-back father to do a lot of things. . . . [After my parents' divorce, neither my brother nor I] had a role model of success, or even a respected male figure to look up to. I think Curtis, being older, was more sensitive to that than I was. But no matter how hard she had to work with him, Mother wouldn't give up.

No matter how close a relationship exists between boys and their mothers, boys naturally search for male figures—for an understanding of what it means to be male. An essential rite of passage for any young boy is psychological separation from his mother so he can discover his masculine self. Some mothers feel so anxious about the need to protect their sons that they discourage them from separating. They view the world as so hostile to black males that they do not allow their sons to develop a sense of healthy maturity, responsibility, or independence. These mothers mean well, but the ramifications of their overprotectiveness can adversely affect their young men's growing sense of who they are and how they fit into the world around them.

Separating from mother is especially tough for a young boy with no adult male guide. If a mother can see that her son's need for a masculine guide is not a rejection of her, she can step back and allow her son the natural exploration of this vital part of him. But if she sabotages her son's efforts to affirm his masculinity, she can set him up for the possibility of acting out this need in an inappropriate way. Mothers who interfere in their son's natural need to separate from them risk creating men who feel unsure of their masculinity and experience tremendous struggles when they try to relate romantically to women.

Robert, a twenty-seven-year-old black man, told me that he spent most of his adolescence trying to figure out what was meant by manhood because his father left the family when he was very young.

"My father never took any initiative with me and my brother," he said. "My mom took care of everything. Sometimes I just wished my dad would show up consistently, but he didn't. I remember my first day at college, moving-in day. I saw other guys with both parents, and I felt bad that my dad didn't come. When money got short at school he would send some, but only after I begged him for it. I was almost put out at the end of freshman year, but as usual Mom came to the rescue. He had nothing to say about what was going on."

Robert says that he has made peace with his past and his father. "I try not to let things about him bother me. I just have to move on. I do know that what I want more than anything is to be a good father when I have kids. I have learned how *not* to do it." He has forgiven his father for not being there when he needed him, and he was most hesitant to appear critical of his mother in any way. Robert gives her unquestioning acclaim for the job she did with him and his brother.

To this day, Robert says that he knows his mother is the standard by which he measures every woman he meets. But it is clear that he is still searching for a missing piece of himself—the view of masculinity that his mother could not provide. Like many young black men who grew up alone with mothers, he is struggling to anchor both the masculine and feminine sides of his personality.

Fear of female dominance is a recurrent theme I hear from many black men who come to me for counseling. The fear is deeply rooted in how they experience their relationships with their mother, grandma, aunt, or other female guardian. Sociologist Nathan Hare and his wife, Julia Hare, in the book *The Endangered Black Family*, explain how this fear of black women begins between a son and his mother:

> Others take up a psychic war with women out of a deep need to be nurtured, seeing every woman they meet as replicas of their mothers who intimidated them in infancy, seemed all-powerful and mysterious, and later withheld goodies and nurturance from their whim . . . Such men see women as an inexhaustible repository or cupboard of nurturance and satisfaction, but, since no woman can replenish, let alone undo, the lost nurturance . . . they are doomed forever to an infantile dissatisfaction and longing, repeating and fighting out all over the unresolved conflicts with their mothers.

James was a forty-year-old black man who had been married several times and felt that most of his lack of success with women was because "they are takers." Because he felt that black women were always taking advantage of him, he unconsciously set up situations in which he took advantage of them—leading them on and never "giving up" his heart to real intimacy. Even though he easily found women to play this game with him, he ended up resenting them, saying they were too weak and dependent to maintain his interest.

James refused to see his own part in his unhappiness. He was a successful businessman and felt proud of what he had achieved in a society with limited opportunities for black men. An only child of a very strong-willed mother, James remembers feeling intensely pressured by her to succeed. His father was a shadowy figure who came around sometimes, but told his son that he couldn't visit more often because of the mother's tirades about his inability to provide for them. James remembers clothes shopping with his mother and having her make all the decisions about what they would buy. She decided what subjects he should study in school, what sports he should pursue, and which girls were okay to date.

At some point during his childhood, James made a decision that no woman would ever again take this kind of control of him. No woman! Harboring all of this resentment toward his mother, he brought his pent-up fear and anger to each romantic relationship. He resisted real intimacy with any woman because he feared that demonstrating real feelings would leave him under her control. He played at being romantic—wining and dining his dates, even being sexually intimate—but refused to be emotionally vulnerable.

Another man, Calvin, related a similar story. He was a forty-five-year-old architect who grew up in a household with a mother he perceived as all-powerful. Calvin's father was present, but deferred all child-rearing responsibilities to the mother. Calvin's most vivid memories of his mother were hearing her rant and rave about the father's failings as a provider. Wanting the good life for her family, she felt that he did not work hard enough or effectively enough to get the family the things she wanted. The neighborhood wasn't good enough, the car wasn't big enough, and she wanted all three of her children to go to private schools.

Calvin recalled his mother as a loving taskmaster, but when he let his guard down it was clear that he felt ambivalent about her. He was upset when she put down his father and ultimately he empathized with his father's precarious status in the home. Calvin felt that his mother's love was conditional on his ability to please her, and even as an adult he made sure to comply with her every wish.

Calvin also tried to please his wife, but she complained that he was emotionally remote. He was so busy making sure his loved ones had material comforts that, according to his wife, he did not "share his feelings." Yet to Calvin, meeting other people's needs *was* expressing love; he equated being needed with being loved, a lesson he learned early from his mother.

Black mothers have to be extremely careful that they do not allow their own unfinished business with men to affect their relationships with their sons. With the raging hostility that passes between black men and women, that is a trap easily fallen into. And women who jealously protect their rights as mothers must let down their guard and allow and encourage men into the child-rearing process. Many men declare that they want to be fathers, but they don't want a woman dictating how that relationship should develop. In some instances, when black women complain that their men are unreliable fathers and that they must protect their children from this disappointment, they are actually reflecting the lesson about black men that they were taught all their lives: "Black men ain't to be trusted."

A black mother with a twenty-three-year-old son of whom she is very proud reluctantly admitted that while they had a wonderfully caring relationship, she now realized that a stable male parent could have made him more independent of her and more confident in himself.

"My son's father did the basics," she said. "We always saw him at the end of the week when he would come around to drop off his child-support payment. There was never any prearranged schedule for when they could spend time together. I saw other women like me having to share parenting with fathers on those every-other-weekend and every-other-holiday schedules, and I secretly was happy that my son's father wasn't interested in this kind of arrangement. I didn't want to be bothered. My son never complained about the situation, so I thought it was fine with him, but it probably had more to do with his not wanting to upset me.

"Now that he is grown, I see how different he is from some of his male friends who had fathers present in the home," she continued. "You know, those kinds of fathers who are right there showing their boys how to be the man of the house, how to be responsible. They learn to imitate their dads in a way that gives them a little more confidence in themselves. As women, I think we are easier on boys, especially if they are all we have. I didn't mind doing things for my son. I enjoyed it. But men aren't always like that with the boys. They are more demanding than we are."

I know the father of this young man, and he confided to me once that he had no idea of how to father anyone. His own father left him when he was young, and remained a hazy figure in his memory. Consequently, when he broke up with his wife, he thought that paying his child support on time and picking up the child occasionally was all a father really needed to do. He also believed that his ex-wife knew best and whatever she asked him to do, he tried to deliver. The problem was that she didn't want real involvement from him. So he was left with no direction—not from his past or from his ex-wife, who rightly felt no responsibility for telling this man how to father his son.

Mothers and Daughters

While black boys must struggle for an identity separate from the mother, identification with her is critical for black girls. Through their relationships with their mothers, girls gain a cognitive understanding of what "goes with" being a woman.

Most black girls grow up seeing their mothers taking care of themselves, even if there is a man present in the home. The girls infer that their own survival will depend upon how well they learn to take care of themselves, too. Many get an early start, taking on the responsibility of running a home very early in life because their mothers must work long hours outside the home. At the same time, they are very aware that their own lives are quite contrary to what they see on television; in their household, no man is providing much guidance or bringing home the bacon. So many black girls grow up obsessed with having what their mothers did not—the fanciful rescuing charmer.

Yet the modeling these girls receive sets them up for future disappointment in their love lives. They are trained, often with the sanction of male family members, to be aggressive, opinionated, and excessively self-reliant. The message they internalize may seem like a harsh one: assertiveness, self-reliance, and responsibility will protect you in a world where a man may be unavailable or unreliable.

As an example of what this message may sound like to young girls, I offer the words of Mudear, the protagonist of Tina McElroy Ansa's novel *Ugly Ways*:

> I tried to tell the girls, tried my best to tell them: a man don't give a damn about you. No matter how much he claim to love you. . . . I never did talk down to my girls the way some grownup folks do with children. I always talked to 'em the way I expected them to be, women. And they understood me, too.

Never did come crying to me with some little silly stuff that they knew I didn't have no interest in. I never could stand a whole lot a' childish crying and whining. . . . I tried to show them how freeing it is to discover that and really live your life by that. . . . "That man don't give a damn 'bout me. . . ." To say that and know it ain't got nothing to do with you, that that's just the way a man is. And when it don't hurt no more, then you free.

Self-reliance is important, but so is the ability to be vulnerable with a mate. A girl's masculine and feminine sides must be in balance in order to allow her to enjoy future emotional interdependence with a man. Of course, a girl must learn to support and speak up for herself. But as I found in my doctoral research on self-efficacy in black women, over-developing traits of self-reliance to the exclusion of more feminine ones can wreak havoc in relationships. Women with dominant masculine sides often seem defensive and wary of getting too close with a man. In turn, some black men experience such black women as too aggressive and bossy, and are put off by their "I can take men or leave them" attitude.

In a paper on black male-female relations in the *Journal of Black Studies*, researcher Clyde Franklin urged a new socialization process for black girls. He urged that "warmth, caring, and nurturance" be stressed in addition to self-sufficiency, assertiveness, and responsibility. Teaching girls a balanced sense of self-reliance is intrinsically worthwhile, but Franklin warned parents not to teach their daughters—directly or not—that they must become self-reliant because black men are intrinsically untrustworthy. "To say 'a nigger man ain't shit,' " said Franklin, "informs any young black female that at least one-half of herself 'ain't shit.' Without a doubt, this strategy teaches self-hate and sets the stage for future black male–black female conflict."

Maggie, a forty-six-year-old marketing executive, took after her mother, who "was like the manager of a huge corporation. Both parents worked, but she believed it was her job to see that babies got fed and dishes and laundry got done, so she delegated. She set up a rotation system of housework for us kids and everybody did everything. She worked from 11 P.M. to 7 A.M., so she was always home when we were up and about, making sure everything got done."

Maggie painted the picture of a busy household with six children.

Because of the size of the family, Maggie experienced a great deal of independence at an early age. Her mother's credo was that each sibling took care of the one next in line, so Maggie was put in charge of her younger sister. She concentrated so much on raising her sister that even into adulthood she felt somewhat alienated from and uninvolved with her other siblings.

Her family was struck early by many tragedies. Three sons were killed in accidents just a couple of years apart. These tragedies strengthened Maggie's own determination to survive. Through a series of impressive career moves, Maggie worked her way up the ladder. From being a teacher, to an educational counselor, to a sales manager, to a marketing executive for a major cable television network, Maggie relentlessly pursued whatever goals she set for herself. Along the way she studied French and put three children through college. She held the reins of her life tightly and was very self-absorbed and controlled. No one ever threw Maggie off her career or social track.

Maggie's mother's toughness and early teaching, she says, sustained her into adulthood. For example, her mother often told her, "If you can think it, you can do it." Yet in part, Maggie's need for control was her way of giving herself mothering that she felt she had lacked as a child.

Maggie's dominating personality did not bode well, however, for her marriage. After her divorce, Maggie told me, "I don't get hyped up about any relationship. Life is easier without men. They demand too much attention and are just not mature enough for me. I deal with life without fear."

Recently Maggie remarried, but not until her new husband assured her that she could continue to work hard to meet her career and personal goals. He had begged her to marry him, even though she insisted there really was no need to do so; she was secure financially and content being single. What was most interesting to me was that her new husband had lost his own mother when he was very young. He subconsciously yearned for a "mommy" and of course Maggie filled that role quite well.

While black women may concentrate a great deal of their energy on rearing strong, independent daughters, the mother-daughter relationship can become so fused that girls are given no opportunity to develop their own unique sense of identity. Still other mothers send this double message: "Be independent, but don't develop an identity that is in contrast with mine. Take care of my emotional insecurities and desire to remain attached." Young women receiving this message can develop a profound subconscious dependency upon their mothers, and feel intense guilt about detaching. Later on, when they need to be comfortable enough with themselves to set boundaries in love relationships, they're at a loss as to how to do it.

This is a setup for black women because it makes attachments with men very precarious situations. On the surface, these women may seem independent and sure of themselves, but inside they are often quaking with uncertainty. They may be overly anxious to bond and to be accommodating, and may not always be discriminating about whom they choose to love. When a crisis develops, these women don't know whom to please—the partner or themselves. Women whose own mothers struggled with men often despair of finding good loving for themselves, for they suspect that most romantic relationships are fated to be unsatisfying and impermanent. Because they are so wary, they often try to control the relationship and conceal their more tender qualities. The pattern often results in disappointing cycles of high hopes followed by rejection, abandonment, and deepening feelings of unworthiness.

Where's Daddy?

An August 1993 issue of *Newsweek* featured a cover story on the growing problem of fatherlessness in the black community. The statistics are staggering: "The institution of marriage has been devastated in the last generation: 2 out of 3 first births to black women under 35 are now out of wedlock. . . . A black child born today has only a 1-in-5 chance of growing up with two parents until the age of 16. Fatherless homes boost crime rates, lower educational attainment and add dramatically to the welfare rolls."

Fathers help mothers provide protection and emotional boundaries for their children. Without the influence of male authority figures during childhood, adult men and women may spend a lifetime in an endless search for masculine approval and/or identity. Psychologist Dr. Earl T.

Braxton, a clinical psychologist who has worked with many black young people, and who is currently the president of an organizational development firm in Pittsburgh, once wrote that in a two-parent family, "the parent of the opposite sex tells the child what kind of person to be, while the parent of the same sex tells the child *how* to be it." Needless to say, for children with absent or silent fathers, a significant part of this equation is lacking, leaving many black children with little understanding of the emotional roles men and women must play in a loving union.

Everyone is sure that fathers are critically important to the emotional development of healthy boys and girls, but fathers are also mysteries on the American family landscape. Writer and journalist Victoria Secunda says in her book *Women and Their Fathers: The Sexual and Romantic Impact of the First Man in Your Life* that "fathers tend to be fantasy figures—feared or adored. There is little in between, no gray area." Secunda takes a courageous and compassionate look at the ways fathers and daughters see each other and themselves, noting that many women have "father hunger"—a continuing need to resolve their attachment to the first man in their lives.

If fathers are fantasy figures in society at large, one can only imagine how fuzzy the picture of father must be in the black community. And there is absolutely no way to talk about relations between black men and women without discussing the impact of the presence or absence of this critical figure in the life of young boys and girls. While much has been written about how missing or silent fathers have a negative impact on the development of young boys, young girls also yearn for a father figure.

Numerous studies point to the fact that a woman's capacity for a mutually loving and sexually fulfilling attachment is directly related to her relationship to her father. Women who are unable to sustain romantic relationships almost always had fathers who could not be counted on, or who were emotionally or physically unavailable when they were growing up. A loving mother is not enough to offset those difficulties.

A missing father can mean a lifetime search for daddy figures in every romantic endeavor. Too many girls grow up not being affirmed by a man, not knowing what it's like to be nurtured, protected, or acknowledged by a paternal figure. As women, they often seek love and closeness in dysfunctional relationships, tolerating distant, nonnurturing men who exhibit behaviors similar to those of their absent or fantasized fathers.

A girl with a missing or silent father never gets to see the emotional give-and-take that is necessary between two adult caregivers. Many years ago I saw this dynamic at work when I was a counselor in a residential group home for adolescent girls. Few had been raised with a father, and I made arrangements to co-lead a support group with Dr. Earl T. Braxton, the psychologist I mentioned earlier, in order to give the girls an opportunity to work on issues with two parent figures. Our work together gave the girls a rare look at nonsexual male-female bonding, balance, and boundaries.

The girls loved watching us work together. They seemed fascinated that a man and a woman were even capable of a nonromantic collaboration. Some persistently asked whether he and I were dating (we weren't) and when we were going to get married (we didn't).

The girls were especially impressed by how well Dr. Braxton and I got along. For example, even if he and I disagreed about something, we could easily agree to disagree, thereby providing the girls with a healthy model of conflict negotiation. Unlike many of the men and women with whom these girls had grown up, Dr. Braxton never stalked out the door in anger, and I never wept and begged him to stay. A disagreement was an opportunity for respectful discussion; it was not a signal to begin battle.

Dr. Braxton was a "hot commodity" in that group home. Some girls acted giddy around him and tried to flirt, some were shy, and virtually all competed for his attention. One girl even shoved her best friend out of the way so she could talk with him first! After our therapy group, I sometimes found myself waiting for him afterwards in the office where we "debriefed"—because the girls didn't want to let him go. He clearly evoked feelings of "father longing," and some girls were visibly sad when he had to leave at the end of the day. He was the only male figure they had a chance to see, and they couldn't get enough of him.

Many of the girls at the home felt that because they were in a group home, they weren't worth much. I will never forget one bright fifteen-year-old who asked me, "Why on earth would you want to be here with bad girls?" When I told her that no one was bad, that some of us just had bad luck, she shrugged her shoulders and rolled her eyes in disbelief. I soon became attached to the girls and started taking small groups of them home with me on weekends. They couldn't believe that I had a husband and a "home with pictures on the wall." It was clear that they were yearning for the same kind of environment—a home and a father they could call their own.

In the black community, and in any community for that matter, it is important to point out that biological parents are not the only men who can provide fathering. Almost any responsible adult male can offer valuable guidance if he is willing to be a consistent presence in a young person's life. School teachers and community center counselors, basketball coaches and other sports leaders, church leaders and Sunday School teachers, friends and neighbors, and, in early adulthood, the military can be positive influences. Many men provide male role modeling for black children through such national programs as Concerned Black Men, Inc., a group of married and single black professional men who are mentors for black children being raised by a single mother, and the Coalition of 100 Black Men, which raises funds for such programs. In addition, there are programs sponsored by women's groups such as LINKS, an organization that adopts schools and works with black teens, and the National Council of Negro Women, which sponsors "family reunions" throughout the black community. We need more of these types of programs so that black boys can develop into positive male citizens, respecting themselves enough to trust and love black women, and so that black girls can avoid the father longing that haunts them with fantasies that no real man can fulfill.

Some black men and women provide guidance and support for children on their own. In his book *Climbing Jacob's Ladder: The Future of the African-American Family*, sociologist Andrew Billingsley cites the experience of a well-to-do black couple:

Kent Amos was a thirty-seven-year old, successful Xerox Corporation executive. His wife, Carmen Harden, was also employed. They had two children, aged sixteen and twelve. Though they could afford the best private high school for their son, they decided to put him in the local high school. . . . In a short time, with the encouragement of his parents, their son began bringing his friends home from school. It was apparent to Kent and Carmen that those children needed help and they elected to give it. . . .

[Kent] quietly designed an after-school program for their son Wesley and his friends in their home. "You are welcome in this house," he said. "Here you will be treated like our own kids. But you'll also be held to the standards we set for them." He also told the youths, "Work hard and get an education. You can be whatever you want to be."

Soon the routine was set. After school a group of boys came to the Amos home for fellowship and parenting, as well as chores, homework, dinner, and recreation and conversation. Amos and Carmen were surrogate parents to them all. Within six years the number of these boys had reached fifty. . . . In 1987 the evening study sessions outgrew the Amos home and moved to the neighborhood school, with the monitoring of the athletic director, Arthur Riddle. After nearly ten years Amos could give the following report of how two individuals can make a difference in the lives of often wayward black youth. Of the fifty members of this augmented family, eighteen had graduated from college, and another eighteen were still in college. Most of the others were employed or in school. Only a few had been lost to the streets.

One black mother told me that when her son reached the age of thirteen, he became obsessed with finding his father, whose whereabouts were unknown to her. When she shared her concern about her teenaged son with a male friend who lived in a distant city, he volunteered to have the boy come for a brief stay. After considering this idea, she felt she had no other viable choice. The boy went, had a wonderful time, and now visits and phones this man regularly. He also became less focused on finding his missing dad.

At a church-sponsored singles male-female session I conducted, a young man rose hesitantly to speak about a desire he had had all his life. He talked about wanting his father to say he loved him. Not until the son lay close to death after a heart attack did his father fulfill his wish. The father came to the hospital, stood by his son's bed, and with great difficulty uttered the words the son had waited so long to hear. As he related the story to the group, his eyes welled with tears.

I was struck by how important the expression of a father's love was to this grown man. I imagined the legions of young black boys who will never hear "I love you" from any significant male, and perhaps never be held or comforted by one. In fact we know that for the majority of young black boys there is no significant intimate male figure in their lives. Is it any wonder that many young black men go into their communities in search of appropriate examples of male leadership, only to find other peers who themselves are at a loss for male guidance? Is it any wonder that so many black men have no idea how to love themselves or how to freely give love to their women and children?

3

The Entitlement Syndrome

But the human animal almost never pursues power without first convincing himself that he is *entitled* to it. And this feeling of entitlement has its own precondition: to be entitled one must first believe in one's innocence, at least in the area where one wishes to be entitled.

—SHELBY STEELE, *The Content of Our Character*

The belief that a partner should make one happy is not uncommon; most men and women entering a romantic relationship hope this will happen. With maturity some couples come to realize that no one person can make them happy all of the time, but other couples struggle with this desire throughout their relationship. Partners have a right to expect honesty, patience, support, cooperation, and most of all respect from each other. What they cannot expect is for someone else to give them a feeling of self-esteem or to make up for past suffering or injustices. Self-fulfillment is possible in a relationship when the partners focus on what is good in the partnership rather than on what is missing.

By the time a couple reaches my office, one or the other has lost hope that this relationship can produce any happiness unless I, the therapist, can fix one of the partners. When they discover that I cannot do this, they wonder whether therapy may be less a solution than a problem: why embark on this journey if the therapist cannot achieve for us what we so ardently desire? When I initiate a discussion of how feelings of emotional entitlement get in the way of many potentially rewarding relationships, most are curious about what this means for them as a couple.

I was hesitant at first to use the word *entitlement* with my clients because it has such a negative connotation in the black community. Many use it to suggest that black people receive benefits in this society that they have not earned. And, of course, I want to avoid having any of my clients feel that a healthy relationship with a good and loving partner is not something they deserve. So I begin any discussion of emotional entitlement very carefully, stressing at the outset that it is not unusual to feel entitled to certain things in life and paramount on this list should be a good relationship. The problem comes in when an individual decides that someone else—specifically a romantic partner—is responsible for fulfilling all of their needs and making up for all of life's inequities. When this kind of thinking occurs one's feeling of emotional entitlement stands in the way of healthy relating.

What I call the entitlement syndrome is a subconscious belief that is manifested as an attitude: "You [my partner] owe me what I feel I should have received—and had the *right* to receive—from my parents and from society." The "entitled" individual is really looking for a partner who will take on a parental role. If parents disappointed the individual during childhood, then in adulthood he or she subconsciously makes the leap that a romantic partner can be the ideal parental replacement. This process is sometimes called "emotional adoption," whereby people expect lovers to give them the emotional support and love they thought was lacking from their parents.

It is important to understand that feelings of loss are quite common among many African Americans. The sense that "something is missing from my life" is often characteristic of many within a family, and may even be passed from one generation to the next. When children grow up hearing their elders say they don't know where the next meal will come from, or they can't pay the rent, or they are suffering from racism and aren't getting their due from society, children often yearn to make matters right once and for all when they become adults. Unfortunately far too many African Americans look outside themselves to fulfill their longing for restitution. It is a way of thinking we in the black community have learned all too well. Consequently, it is no wonder that many black individuals expect that their romantic partner will provide them with the emotional security that can come only from within.

The accompanying graph may help to visualize the multilayered

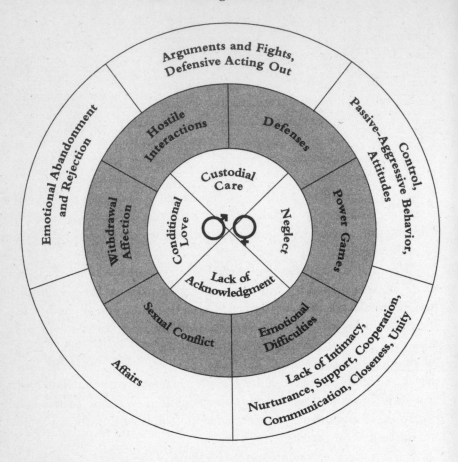

The Entitlement Syndrome

Inner Ring: Experience of childhood environment
Middle Ring: Effect of childhood environment on romantic relations
Outer Ring: Emotional or behavioral reactions to unfulfilled expectations

concept of entitlement. The innermost ring represents childhood, when entitlement problems first take root. How a child is cared for shapes his or her sense of personal worth and feelings of entitlement. I always ask clients for detailed descriptions of how and by whom they were reared, how love and attention were demonstrated, and how they were shown that they mattered as an individual. The types of caregiving shown in the graph are those that clients with entitlement issues most frequently describe.

Custodial care provides the basics of living, such as food, shelter, and clothing, but offers little real emotional involvement from the caregivers. For example, a mother struggling to hold two jobs in order to feed and house her children may have little energy left for holding, hugging, or cuddling when the children experience the inevitable hurts and frustrations that accompany growing up. The children may feel "taken care of," but not necessarily emotionally secure or loved. They do not feel affirmed as unique individuals.

In the novel *Mama*, Terry McMillan described a mother who tended to her children's basic needs, but offered little in the way of overt affection:

Mildred's heart was signaling her to reach over and pull her oldest daughter inside her arms. But she couldn't. A plastic layer had grown over that part of Mildred's heart and it refused to let her act on impulse. She never showed too much attention because that made her feel weak. And she hated feeling weak because that made her vulnerable. Who would be there to pick up the pieces if she let herself break down? Mildred felt she had to be strong at all times and at all costs.

Freda wanted her mama to hug her, but she was afraid to make the first move. She didn't want Mildred to think she was being a baby about this whole thing. At that moment, Freda couldn't remember Mildred ever hugging her, or any of them. The two of them sat there stiffly, like starched shirts, but underneath, Mildred and Freda mourned for themselves.

Most black mothers are very nurturing, and if they end up being "custodial" it is rarely a deliberate choice; rather, they are so consumed by the stresses of caring for a family that they have little left to give. Often, this seemingly harsh message is delivered unconsciously to children. Additionally, some parents are not aware of the need to do more. They really believe that if they keep their kids fed, clothed, and sheltered, it's enough. From a child's perspective, of course, such basic care is not sufficient; it does not address the needs of the heart.

Another source of entitlement feelings is a lack of acknowledgment during childhood. An unacknowledged child might feel like a fixture in the household, unnoticed for any particular talents and strengths. For example, a bright child may get little reinforcement for his or her exceptional scholastic aptitude. The family might focus only on how well the child performs household chores or other family obligations—and never mention academic achievements. The parent or guardian may have said such things as "I love all my children," but ignored individual children's specific skills and personality traits.

Conditional love is based solely on performance. Rather than being loved unconditionally ("I love you no matter what"), children are rewarded with love and support only if they meet certain conditions, such as doing well in school, excelling in sports, or doing housework to perfection. If children do not live up to the parents' expectations, they risk being ignored or left standing on the sidelines while other siblings get all the praise. Such children are trained to believe that they must prove themselves worthy of love. Ultimately they become adults who believe they must always meet standards set by others. They do not fully develop a sense of who they are.

The most devastating type of parental behavior shown in the graph is neglect, which is a form of abuse. Neglected children are constantly in need of both the basics of living and the emotional support all human beings need to develop healthy egos. They may spend a lifetime looking for the nurturance and attention they never received during childhood, or may continue into adulthood the destructive behaviors they developed as "survival skills."

The graph's middle ring illustrates how individuals' reactions to how they were raised are transferred to romantic partners. For instance, an individual who suffered from a lack of personal acknowledgement may have great difficulty sharing his or her true self with another because of a shallow and unstable sense of self. An emotional or romantic connection evokes a great deal of anxiety and a deeply felt sense of vulnerability. If custodial care was the mainstay of their upbringing, their emotional makeup might be characterized by perpetual mistrust and a rigid defense system to protect themselves and keep others from getting too close. Conditional love makes children fear rejection and abandonment. Later, as adults, they may feel terribly unsure of their partners' affection and commitment and need constant demonstrations of love.

The graph's outer ring represents emotional and behavioral patterns that entitlement-minded individuals use in their adult relationships to attempt to receive what they feel they must have in order to feel emotionally whole and secure. Arguments and fights might mask the real pain and sadness one feels when a partner cannot fill an emotional void. Controlling, passive-aggressive behavior is often used to pay back a disappointing partner who has not come through in the way expected. Another form of payback is the romantic affair—which can also be a means of finding acknowledgment to assuage some old emotional wounds. Another method is the withdrawal of affection or communication as a way of expressing a hurt or disappointment.

Emotional abandonment and rejection can be the ultimate weapons against a partner who cannot deliver the emotional goods. Entitlement-minded individuals may, for example, continuously set up scenarios where they can do the leaving, and thus have a ready excuse for the lack of consistent love and affection in their lives. Rejection can also come from the partner who has diligently tried to satisfy but ultimately gives up what is essentially a losing game.

Romantic love does not give anyone the right to be rescued by another. Partners should support and love each other, but they cannot be responsible for the other person's life struggles—a reality that an entitled individual very often can find profoundly frustrating and even infuriating.

The Assumptions of Entitlement

Entitlement wishes come disguised in various forms; sometimes real needs are so well hidden that it takes weeks or months of therapy for individuals to recognize what they are really trying to get from their partner. I've learned to "listen between the lines" of my clients' arguments and stories for underlying assumptions—misguided beliefs that can set up cycles of angry, disappointing relationships. Among the assumptions I hear clients express are:

If you loved me, you would . . .

This statement is perhaps the most common I hear. It is used to describe what a person's partner must do or say in order to make the individual feel loved, wanted, and needed. The problem with this assumption is that it is often unclear to the partner what is really being asked for. For example, a wife may always want to know her husband's whereabouts. She feels he is obligated to give his wife this information; if he loved her he should be willing to comply with her demand even though it makes him feel crowded and resentful. What she is really concerned about is probably a great deal more substantive. She more than likely fears abandonment or rejection, but cannot articulate this feeling, even to herself.

I do everything for you, why can't you do everything for me . . .

This statement signals the desire for a quid pro quo relationship, an equal exchange. For example, women often tell me, "I gave this man everything I had to give, but he does little in return." These women are making the assumption that their choice to "give everything" should in turn make the partner feel obligated to fill up their emotional void. If he does not buy in on this notion, only disappointment can result.

The world is unfair, my partner should know how difficult it is for me . . .

Some black men operate on this assumption in their romantic liaisons. They firmly believe that black women "owe them" because the world limits black men's aspirations and attainments. They also erroneously believe that black women have a much easier time of it, therefore they should go the extra mile to be supportive and take care of men's needs. Some black women also operate with this assumption because they have been raised to believe that they are responsible for the well-being of everyone in their lives. However, while taking care of everyone's needs they secretly long for their partner to recognize their plight and make things up to them.

If you won't give me what I want, somebody else will . . .

This veiled threat is acted out in numerous ways by people whose entitlement wishes are unfulfilled. For example, a man who is feeling lonely or neglected because his wife is too busy may begin to make demands that seem silly or childish to her. He may want his head rubbed before bed or a special meal on a night when she is utterly exhausted. He wants to see if she will comply with his wishes. If she doesn't, retaliation is sure to follow. He may storm out of the house and stay out all night, or begin dropping hints about a woman in the office who thinks he is attractive. This dynamic is by no means the sole province of men; women act it out as well.

When do I get mine? . . .

I often hear this kind of statement from black women who feel that life's demands and responsibilities rest awkwardly on their shoulders: "When is he going to take care of something? When can I get a break from being the responsible one?" Essentially they are saying: "Surely my man should want to relieve my burdens and make me feel better about myself." Clearly, waiting to get what you think is rightfully yours can be a huge obstacle in a relationship, especially when your partner doesn't understand what you really want or need.

What my parents didn't give me, I will get from you . . .

This thought is almost never openly articulated. Instead it is a closely held belief that guides a person's actions within the relationship. Men or women operating under this assumption are always on the lookout for "this magical thing" that is missing from their lives, even if they can't articulate what it is exactly. These people fully intend to receive this special something from their chosen mate. If this magical wish is not assigned to a partner, it may be to a therapist or friend.

What I got from my parents, you better keep giving me . . .

Closely connected to the above assumption is the feeling that whatever parents provided, either emotionally or materially, should be continued in the exact same manner by a romantic partner. This can be a critical stumbling block, especially for young couples. For example, many young black women want their mates to be able to provide economically at a level equal to their parents, not realizing how many years it took for their parents to achieve economic security. In a similar vein, some black men expect their mates to not only be "like mama" in appearance and personality but to also behave almost exactly as mama would. I have even heard stories about husbands asking their wives to take cooking lessons so they can prepare meals exactly as their mothers did.

Settling Accounts: The Emotional Investment

The struggle to gain or obtain what was not emotionally sufficient in one's past is often carried out in a process I like to call the *emotional investment account*. People make emotional investments in their partners as one would in a savings account, fully planning to get interest back. However, they often find that there's no payoff to be had when they try to cash in. Then they feel used, angry, and vengeful. These investments may be made on a variety of levels: social, economic, emotional, or physical.

Social investments might include escorting a partner to elegant parties or wining and dining in an extravagant way. Economic investing is when money is used to build a partner's obligation. Always being there, or mothering and smothering are examples of emotional investments made with the unspoken expectation that a return will be forthcoming. Physical investments include sexual behavior that is designed to hold a partner's attention and excitement even when little else may be happening in the relationship. (This approach is discussed further in chapter 6.)

The greater one's investment in a partner, the higher the return expected. The problem is that the partner may not have a clue about these expectations and may accept the investment without really understanding that some kind of payback is considered due. Even worse, the partner may be incapable of providing that which is desired. More often than not, the investment is made without the terms of the contract ever being verbalized. The result is an unconscious contract that is unfavorable for both parties.

At a singles workshop I conducted at a suburban Maryland church a few years back, a discussion about the current state of black male-female relations was highlighted by the perceptive comments of a young black man. He was impressively articulate and direct about what he felt needed to happen so that black men and women might begin to better understand each other. I remember him well because the men in my seminars are not always so comfortable expressing their feelings. In fact, he pointed out to the group that black men needed to reach into themselves and learn how to feel so they could become better partners and more caring fathers. As usual, the women had no problem vocalizing what they wanted from men, and in many cases theirs was an "if it can't be this way, I don't want it" approach. He talked with some humor about black women walking around with a checklist and eliminating men who didn't score high enough on the list. Everyone laughed, not realizing how very serious he was.

When I left the seminar, I was struck by how the women seemed to regard having a man as a natural right; if they invested enough time and energy they could obtain the exact package they had imagined all their lives. Yet none of the women in this group had considered this well-spoken young man as a potential partner. He wasn't the smartest dresser nor would he be considered handsome by conventional standards, but clearly he was earnest about wanting to find a black woman to love. I wondered why this wasn't enough. Many black men and women are so consumed with the image of the fantasy partner they feel entitled to that they are unable to realistically evaluate the person before them. They keep looking for the perfect person who will make them feel complete and meet emotional needs that have been neglected for a lifetime.

A teacher named Sarah, who is now well into her sixties, once told me that if she had felt entitled to a handsome, rich black man, she'd still be unmarried. When she was twenty-eight years old, reality hit home. She realized that it was more important to have someone healthy, employed, and of good character than the mate of her dreams. Sarah feels lucky that she avoided the mindless games and fantasies some of her friends experienced. Determined that entitlement fantasies would not keep her from reaching her goal of having a partner with whom to share her life, she eventually married a working-class man and had three children with him. To this day, Sarah and her man are still married and enjoying a healthy, fulfilling relationship.

When "Big Daddy" Meets "His Baby"

To further examine what entitlement looks like and how it creates untold tension and conflict for couples, let's look at the experience of Kwasi and Ebony.

Married for ten years, Kwasi and Ebony were desperately trying to stay together, but fights and general feelings of discontent had driven them apart. Kwasi was tired of his wife's constant need for rescuing. Ebony expected him to help her with the children and with household responsibilities even though she did not work outside of the home. She also spent money recklessly, running up every charge card they had. Kwasi, on the other hand, avoided going home as much as possible. When he wasn't working well into the night, he hung out in local clubs looking for women who were interested in "fun and games."

Both Kwasi and Ebony felt entitled to "special" attention and believed that a romantic partner should make up to them whatever was missing in childhood. When Ebony's fantasies were not met, she screamed her disappointment. Then Kwasi withdrew his affection and assistance because he was tired of always giving. Ebony firmly believed that it should be his job to take care of her. Over the years, Kwasi had reinforced this belief by making all of the family decisions. It was a familiar role for him. He was very young when his father left him and his mother. It wasn't long before he and his mom had formed an alliance against the world. She relied heavily upon her young son, and he responded to her needs, wanting never to let her down. Kwasi soon learned to play the role of a young father figure who helped his mother with daily challenges.

Ebony came from a large family where child rearing was a loose operation at best. Both parents worked long hours at menial jobs just to provide the basics of food and shelter. She remembered being at home much of the time without either parent while an older sibling was left in charge. She understood that her parents needed to work hard, but she fantasized a lot about "the perfect family." She often imagined sitting on her daddy's lap, talking over the day's events or going on an outing with her mom where the two of them could talk about special things. These fantasies began to dominate her thinking, and now she was determined to have some replication of the images in her head.

As adults, Kwasi and Ebony were reenacting their childhood scenarios. Ebony had grown up physically, but emotionally she was stuck in the child stage. She was self-absorbed and driven by the desire to be noticed, appreciated, and gratified by others. Her anger and hostility were turned inward, but expressed through her demands of what her partner should provide for her. Ebony unwittingly operated with the entitlement assumption "If you loved me, you would . . . ," while Kwasi was a classic case of the assumption "When do I get mine?" He was used to being the rescuer and playing "Big Daddy." His insecure ego made him long to be reaffirmed as a powerful man, so he attached himself to a woman who needed constant attention. He had developed what psychologists call a grandiose personality—a person who overestimates his abilities to please others in order to elevate his self-esteem and his sense of masculinity.

The irony of the situation is this: the more Ebony believed she could obtain from Kwasi those things that she was denied in her childhood, and the more Kwasi believed he could provide it, the more intense their battles became. Ebony needed to come to terms with the fact that she would never have the "perfect family" she dreamed of as a child. And Kwasi needed to understand that every time he pretended he could accommodate his wife's fantasy, only to pull away in the end, he was teasing her while at the same time supporting her unrealistic expectations. Ultimately this "action-reaction" scenario set up disappointment for both, leading to a deterioration of their relationship.

Many individuals are like Kwasi and Ebony, continually playing out the same self-defeating scenarios. The intensity of their connection convinces both partners that they are in love, no matter how bitter the fighting becomes. Neither partner understands that the intensity is really desperation, an attempt to gain access to the positive bonding with a parental figure that they were denied during childhood. Kwasi and Ebony both believed that their marriage could make up for the conditional love and lack of acknowledgment that they suffered as children.

I remind couples like Ebony and Kwasi that they must stop replaying old internalized messages from childhood. Children have little sophistication, and often draw inaccurate conclusions about what they experience. If they are treated negatively, children may infer that they are not worthy of love. As adults, they brace themselves for the disappointment they feel is inevitable in their romantic relationships.

Many black couples relate to each other as "parent-adult" or "child-adult," causing either great expectations or tremendous disappointment when the partner is unable to fulfill entitlement needs. I use Eric Berne's

	Ebony	Kwasi
Parent Person with rescue fantasies of taking care of other person's needs to gain power *Independent*	♀ **Super Mom**	♂ **Big Daddy**
Adult Emotionally balanced adult, able to take care of own needs *Interdependent*	♀ **Adult**	♂ **Adult**
Child Demanding to have needs met by another person *Dependent*	♀ **Baby Ebony**	♂ **Baby Kwasi**

Entitlement Fantasy

Relationship Analysis

transactional analysis model to explain this dynamic and to help individuals understand what a healthier connection should feel like.

The partner's emotional imbalance keeps them polarized, but both play dysfunctional roles in order to sustain their mutual dependency. Often one partner operates as the dependent one while the other operates as the independent parent, causing tremendous anxiety and resentment. They do this to obtain basic unmet needs.

Individuals who operate with an entitlement syndrome behave as the baby or child in the relationship. They need and expect to be taken care of by the other person. They feel that relationships are supposed to give them the unconditional love they deserve.

People who feel a strong need to operate like a parent are more comfortable in a control position. They may also be perpetuating the familiar role of being "the responsible one" that they might have played within their family during childhood. Some children are placed in the role of "peacemaker" or "voice" for the parents. To take care of themselves and have happy parents, they act like the coordinator of the parents' relationship. As adults, these individuals do not feel safe in a relationship where power is shared; this is an unfamiliar role. The best arrangement for romantic partners is when both are operating in the adult state. This role is designed to foster equality, mutual sharing, and healthy acceptance of the partner's traits.

Ebony and Kwasi worked intensively to get their relationship on a solid foundation. They attended sessions for about eight months, working on the many issues that are related to entitlement. Ebony became able to face the painful reality that Kwasi was not in her life solely to rescue her from all the things she couldn't handle herself. She began taking more responsibility for her own happiness and security. For example, she managed her own budget and paid her bills without Kwasi's help. She also became involved in a few community projects where she made new friends and developed new interests. Because she placed fewer inappropriate demands upon her husband, he was less defensive giving what was realistically in his power to give. He began coming home earlier and feeling less defensive with his wife. Consequently, both partners felt less burdened by the relationship.

The situation between Kwasi and Ebony reminds me of an exercise I conducted at a workshop on healthy coupling during which the group attempted to lift up a man—and keep him up. The idea was to have each person feel what it's like to support the weight of another person. The volunteer group of five men and women hoisted up the man, laughing all the while. But when I encouraged them to keep holding him, the laughter stopped and the huffing and puffing began. Someone finally said "He's too heavy." Several said they feared dropping him or they feared disappointing him. Others admitted they were getting tired and wanted someone else to "take the weight." This is an excellent way to illustrate how continually holding up another person can become an awesome responsibility and burden.

When "The Rescuer" Won't Rescue

Another couple in therapy presented problems of entitlement similar to Kwasi and Ebony. Alberta was twenty-eight years old and Ben was twenty-nine. Alberta had initiated the counseling, and Ben clearly did not want to be in my office. He was tense and hostile, and announced, "I'm just here to keep Alberta quiet. I don't think we need to be here."

Alberta opened the discussion, "Ben and I have been seeing each other for a couple of years. I'm really in love with him, and I'm pregnant, and I want this relationship to work out. I am not terminating the pregnancy."

Ben shuffled uncomfortably in his chair.

"I have other plans for this phase of my life," he said. "I'm just getting started at my job at an auto repair shop. Now Alberta's trying to get me settled down before I'm ready. Everything's moving too fast. Our relationship was good the way it was, and I thought she felt the same way. When she told me she was pregnant, I was shocked. She had told me she was taking birth control pills."

When I questioned Alberta about birth control she became agitated and said defensively, "I decided to give my body a rest."

Ben added that although he felt an obligation to the baby, he wanted to distance himself from her.

Despite this statement, I sensed that Ben really cared about Alberta; that he consented to return for another session confirmed my feeling.

As therapy continued, I learned more about Alberta and Ben's backgrounds. Alberta had always wanted a traditional family, and cited *The Cosby Show* as her ideal. Yet her upbringing was far from traditional. Alberta had been raised by her grandmother while her mother, who was unmarried, went to college. When Alberta's mother married, she reclaimed her daughter. Alberta was in junior high school. Although her mother had visited from time to time, Alberta had often lived in a state of steady—and unfulfilled—expectation that she would live with her mother again soon.

Alberta loved her grandmother dearly, and felt disloyal even acknowledging how painful her mother's leaving had been for her. And although she loved her stepfather, she mourned never knowing her own father.

When Alberta met Ben, she saw in him an opportunity to recreate the family she had dreamed about as a young girl. Ben came from a traditional two-parent family, and Alberta assumed that he would want to replicate it—with her. Yet what Alberta did not know was that when Ben was a child, he had resented his mother's constant demands that he help with his siblings. His father held two jobs and was rarely home. When his father was around, he was too tired to be emotionally available to his young son. Now Ben, who had looked forward to earning a living and being free of responsibility to others for a while, saw that his girlfriend, like his mother, wanted to hold him accountable to a child he had not planned. He was unwilling to submit once again to what he saw as female domination.

Through therapy, Alberta gradually gave up the *Cosby* fantasy and acknowledged that she'd had no right to assume that Ben would make her fantasy come true. Ben agreed to negotiate with Alberta about how much responsibility he would take for their child. He said he would not be forced into marriage, but he would support her through pregnancy and delivery, contribute to their son's child-care costs, and faithfully keep to the visitation schedule. As Alberta became less controlling, Ben felt more in control of himself and more inclined to assume what he called his "manly duties." Their relationship eventually became so much more harmonious, in fact, that not long ago I received an invitation to their wedding.

When individuals are entangled in the entitlement syndrome, it can be difficult to unravel all of the issues. Surface concerns—such as who makes the most money or who does the most housework—take on greater importance than they deserve because neither person wants or knows how to dig beneath the surface to find out what is really happening between them. Breaking the dysfunctional cycles between black men and women requires a willingness, however, to face these fears in order to uncover the real reasons for disappointment or frustration. It means confronting the demons that keep one from feeling whole inside. It means letting go of feelings that one is entitled to "compensation" from others. But most of all it means understanding that a mate cannot and should not be assigned the role of savior. Surviving in this country requires too much energy in itself to take on the rescuing of other adults. When an individual accepts the responsibility for his or her own happiness, he or she can relate to another as a whole person rather than an "entitled" person.

When Giving Doesn't Get What You Want

Emotional deprivations, both personal and societal, begin to fade in memory as the years go by. Unwittingly, people often learn to mask their neediness by creating a persona they feel will attract those most likely to give them what they secretly long for and want.

Vanessa was a single thirty-year-old law student who had a long-standing problem maintaining relationships with men. She liked older men and admitted that she was very demanding of her partners. It was clear to me that Vanessa's family background had created some emotional deprivation that she was now trying to make up for in her romances.

Vanessa was the youngest of five children. Her father was an alcoholic who abandoned the family when she was five years old. Her mother struggled to keep them together, and ended up on welfare when she couldn't make it alone. To add to Vanessa's abandonment issues, the mother allowed the father to come and go in her life for several years, causing Vanessa to suffer serial abandonment by a parent. Her story is typical of how a sense of entitlement can build until every romantic encounter is seen as a chance to fill an emotional void.

VANESSA: I guess when my parents were together our family was what you would call middle class. When they split up, my mom had to go on welfare because my dad just disappeared and was in and out of our lives at his convenience.

AUDREY: So basically, he abandoned the family. He wasn't interested in providing financial support, let alone emotional support. So your mother went on welfare to cope.

VANESSA: Yes. Then she started working, which meant no more welfare, and no medical insurance, so it was always a struggle.

AUDREY: What was that like for you? Do you remember?

VANESSA: I remember always wondering what we would eat, if the house would be ours to stay in, and whether my mother would get tired and leave us, too. All of us started working different odd jobs in the neighborhood, probably from the time we were about ten.

AUDREY: That must have been scary for you, not knowing what would happen from day to day.

VANESSA: Yes. Because my dad was very strange. He would migrate back and forth between Pennsylvania and South Carolina, which was his home. I think his movements were unstable because he was an alcoholic. And whenever he would come into town, my mom didn't want to break off our relationship with our father, so she allowed him to see us whenever he wanted to. He would say he was coming by to take us out, and she wouldn't fight him on it, even though he wasn't supporting us.

AUDREY: Do you remember how you felt about his visits?

VANESSA: What I remember most was when he would say he was coming to town for Easter dinner or whatever, and we would, all five of us, get all clean and shiny and make sure we were on our best behavior, waiting for our dad to come take us out. And then he just wouldn't show up at all. So we would sit there, waiting, until about ten or eleven at night.

AUDREY: Sounds like you were disappointed over and over by him.

VANESSA: Yes. But as hard as it was for me, I think it was harder for my two brothers. My one brother, who is a year older than I am, he just worshiped my dad.

AUDREY: Do you think your brother needed to identify with your dad?

VANESSA: Yes, he longed for a daddy. For years and years, no matter how many times our dad disappointed us, my brother always defended his behavior.

AUDREY: He defended him?

VANESSA: Yes. Defended him whenever we would get down on him and cry and complain about him. My brother always defended him. To this day, he still does that.

AUDREY: Sounds like he idealized your dad. Did any of your brothers have any difficulty and act out the abandonment in their lives as a result of your father's drinking—did any of them end up drinking or on drugs themselves? Or did they go to the extreme and become "super" responsible?

VANESSA: My brother—in fact, everyone in my family—has had some sort of alcohol or drug problem, except for me. I've never even experimented with any sort of drug, just because I was the youngest and I could see what they all went through. My brother Andy is in jail right now on a drug charge.

AUDREY: So they not only identified with their father's addiction, they also acted out their sense of unworthiness and shame because they were abandoned. They punished themselves. Did you assign yourself to be the responsible one in the family?

VANESSA: Yes. I'm actually the first college graduate in my entire family. We're talking extended family and everything. It sort of kept me driven. I just couldn't see where I would go if I didn't succeed in school. I'm always trying to recreate myself. Whenever I see a problem, I'm just always trying to be a better person. And I think because of my family I see what happens when you don't take the time to see why you're doing certain things.

AUDREY: You know, sometimes a person who grows up in an alcoholic family will try to take care of other people by encouraging dependency and giving too much.

VANESSA: I hadn't thought about that, but I would certainly agree with it. I always find myself giving constantly to others—I always thought I was a person who was just very big-hearted and loved to do things for men. But I am realizing now, just hearing you say that, that I probably am not just so big-hearted, but I'm trying to win them over so they will stay with me.

AUDREY: Yes, your earlier dependency needs for love and belonging have not been sufficiently met. And you need to prove to yourself that you deserve someone who keeps his word and will not leave you. In the long run the guy ultimately feels seduced by the caring (because he is also dependent), but realizes that if you are also dependent, he will not get his needs met. He may feel compelled to protect himself and will become scared and pull away from you. This further reinforces the belief system or emotional message going in your head. This message says "to love is to lose." Or "to love is to be abandoned." It's like a self-fulfilling prophecy. You subconsciously expect to be left, so you consciously play this out. You are trying to control what was not manageable in your childhood. Because I would imagine that little five-year-old girl who waited many an evening for her father to come for her experienced a lot of disappointment and pain. As a child you had to block the anxiety, anger, and pain, but now as an adult you're trying to work this out through others.

VANESSA: Yes. My father's patterns of being in and out of our lives even continued up through my college years.

AUDREY: That was the other question I was going to ask you. How often was he in and out of your life?

VANESSA: When we were younger it was more frequently—probably about once a year. But I'd say after I was about sixteen or seventeen, it would be maybe every two or three years we'd see him. And the last time I saw him was my senior year of undergrad, which was about three years ago. And since that time I have not laid eyes on him.

AUDREY: Did he come to the school?

VANESSA: When I was in college, he showed up at my mom's house. He was apparently doing well and living in Boston. He just wanted to be back in our lives. And he was in our lives for about a month—a period when he had a phone number, we could talk to him every day. He came over and gave me a lot of money and promised to buy me a car. He said he was back in our lives for good, and apologized for everything he had done. That lasted for about a month. And then contact with him broke off again and we had trouble reaching him at his number. One night, I guess it was about one A.M., he called me at school. He had promised to buy the car, but he couldn't deliver.

AUDREY: It seems you wanted to give him another chance to clean up the mess he had created in your life. You continued to hope he would finally demonstrate his love for you.

VANESSA: Right. And I don't know how exactly it happened, but the conversation got kind of bitter. I was like the baby listening to daddy, letting him make all his excuses, and I forgave him and forgave him. And then he started—I don't know, I guess he had started drinking again. And he said, "You know, I feel so bad. I'm just going to end it all. I'm just—I think I should just commit suicide." For about an hour he went on that way. I kept crying and saying, "Dad, don't do that. We love you."

The conversation ended because I got really mad after a while that I kept trying to save him, I guess like I do now with the men in my life.

AUDREY: It sounds like you learned early to be an enabler and protect others. You learned to be responsible for others and not for yourself. How has this affected your relationships with men?

VANESSA: I've always had an attraction for older men.

AUDREY: Older men?

VANESSA: In undergrad, I had a two-year relationship with one of the professors. I just always thought, "Oh, well, I'm just very liberal, I'm just more mature than my peers." But I don't think it's really that. I think I long for a mature person in my life who's responsible and responsive.

AUDREY: So what's the pattern now with the men in your life?

VANESSA: Over the last year, I've had one long-term relationship and a few dates. I've really only had two relationships that went beyond dating in my whole life. I thought they were going to develop into full, long relationships. And now that I look back—I guess—the breaking factor of all these relationships was when I would have a fit of anger about them not showing up, or calling me at the last minute to cancel a date or something like that.

AUDREY: Did they remind you of your father and mother's inconsistency?

VANESSA: Right. And I thought I was justified. I believed my man should put me first. They shouldn't do this to me. I guess I got a series of bad advice from girlfriends who thought it was okay for me to do what I was doing. So I always left the relationship thinking, "Well, I stood up for myself. I was right. To hell with him if he doesn't want to put me first." And now I don't think my behavior was so normal, or so rational.

Resolving childhood traumas can force some individuals to recreate similar scenarios throughout their life in an attempt to gain mastery over this particular issue once and for all. For example, Vanessa's disappointment with her father's inability to attend to her needs compelled her to get involved with men who also disappointed her in an attempt to conquer her past struggle with the original loved one. She either got involved with men who could not be available to her, or attracted needy men who felt entitled to unconditional love from her. She was trying to rewrite her emotional history.

It's difficult to trust anyone when your first loved ones were not dependable and when they needed more from you than they could give back. When the first woman and man in one's life made promises that they didn't keep, one may decide never to be in that position again. Vanessa received the message: "Daddies aren't dependable, so don't depend on men. Enjoy them, engage them, but don't put yourself in a position where you become dependent on them." From her mother, Vanessa learned that when women are victimized they often make sacrifices that affect both themselves and their children.

As a child, Vanessa did not receive sufficient emotional support to feel worthy and accepting of herself. So in her adult relationships she would give, give, give, because she thought this would guarantee love and appreciation in return. She was stuck in a cycle of entitlement, but she didn't have to be. She had to learn to trust herself and others, learn to forgive her parents, and come to terms with the expectations she had imposed on the men in her life.

4

It's a Man Thing

I don't think it off the wall to speculate that most of the problems between men and women are related to a man's panic in the face of a woman's anger.

—DR. FRANK PITTMAN

Many African-American men seem to search their whole lives long for a working definition of masculinity—a way to preserve their pride and lessen their pain in an unjust society. Their struggle brings to mind the inscrutable face of Denzel Washington in his Academy Award–winning role as Riff, the rebellious runaway slave, in the movie *Glory*. I will never forget his forbidding stance and defiant look when he is beaten repeatedly. Riff tries with all his might to show no emotion, bitterly flaunting his ability to take his punishment "like a man." The scene is emblematic of the dilemma facing modern black men, many of whom also believe that withholding displays of emotion will protect them from feeling in an unfeeling world.

Black men are constantly grappling with such questions as: How can I reduce the chances of feeling vulnerable if I show my pain or rage? Isn't it better to remain impassive to the world? Why can't others see how risky it is to expose my feelings? Most of all, Why can't black women realize that I'll be taken advantage of if I let my guard down? This last question is particularly important to black men who worry a great deal about how to protect themselves emotionally from black women. I sense this worry in many of my male clients; they want some assurances from me that as a black woman I can be sensitive to their problems.

I often wish that I could share with some of my female clients the depth of sensitivity that I hear from black men in the privacy of my office. In my role as a therapist I get an inside look at the psychological world of black men that most black women never see. Even if they are unable to articulate their ambivalence about black women to me in concrete terms, I can tell the men's concerns by some of the questions they ask me. Can black women be fair to a black man and also love him unconditionally? Can she listen to his cares and concerns and be objective? Is he entitled to her emotional support under any circumstances, since the world is so hostile to his goals and aspirations? These are complex questions and I try to answer them honestly. I tell black men that they are entitled to respect, support, and caring, but that love is a two-way street. They also have to be prepared to respect, support, and care in return.

The intense questioning I receive from my black male clients doesn't surprise me. Black men have an extreme hypersensitivity to black women, and because of this, many decide to close themselves off emotionally. I find that most black men maintain an "on-alert" status around black women. Some shut down their vulnerable "feminine" side and overdevelop a macho persona, hoping that their veneer of cool will hide their feelings of emotional neediness, humiliation, and frustration. Everyone employs certain emotional defenses in life, but some men become so *overdefended* that even in their love relationships they are unable to let down their guard. A T-shirt slogan sums up their attitude: "It'a a man thing; you wouldn't understand." The real message is as thorny as porcupine quills: "Keep out. My emotions are unavailable to you."

A Wary Freedom

Black women can relate to and understand Denzel Washington's character in *Glory* because we all know that the harshness of slavery required extraordinary survival skills. What many black women have difficulty understanding is that some of these same psychological dynamics—particularly the need to mask humiliation and frustration—are at work for the men in their lives. Black men are no longer slaves, but they still take plenty of beatings—educational, economic, and social. Although many black men do achieve success, countless others lack adequate education and employment opportunities. The preponderance of single-mother homes, as discussed in chapter 2, deprives many boys of the male role models that could help guide them to a secure and productive adulthood. Guns, drugs, and bitter social conditions contribute to a horrifying statistic: the leading cause of death for black men aged eighteen to twenty-four is homicide.

Yet even men who get a decent education, have jobs, and are economically stable cannot escape the everyday insults that are part of the black man's experience in America. Most boys become aware of racism during childhood, and by their teen years many experience it firsthand. Brent Staples, a black editor for the *New York Times*, describes a difficult and impoverished childhood in his memoir *Parallel Time*. Staples managed to extricate himself from his hardscrabble neighborhood by enrolling in a military college. His subsequent enrollment in graduate school at the University of Chicago should have been a peak experience in his life, an affirmation of his hard work and intelligence. Yet it was in Chicago that Staples first became aware that many people felt frightened when they saw him on the street—simply because he was a young black man. Staples had never thought of himself as a sight to be feared:

> Couples locked arms or reached for each other's hand when they saw me. Some crossed to the other side of the street. People who were carrying on conversations went mute and stared straight ahead, as though avoiding my eyes would save them. This reminded me of an old wives' tale: that rabid dogs didn't bite if you avoided their eyes. The determination to avoid my eyes made me invisible to classmates and professors whom I passed on the street.
>
> It occurred to me for the first time that I was big. I was 6 feet 1½ inches tall, and my long hair made me look bigger. . . . I tried to be innocuous but didn't know how. The more I thought about how I moved, the less my body belonged to me; I became a false character riding along inside it. I began to avoid people. I turned out of my way into side streets to spare them the sense that they were being stalked. I let them clear the lobbies of buildings before

I entered, so they wouldn't feel trapped. Out of my nervousness I
began to whistle . . . popular tunes from the Beatles and Vivaldi's
"Four Seasons." The tension drained from people's bodies when
they heard me. . . .

Then I changed. . . . Once I had hustled across the street,
head down, trying to seem harmless. Now I turned brazenly into
the headlights and laughed. Once across, I paced the sidewalk,
glaring until the light changed. They'd made me terrifying. Now
I'd show them how terrifying I could be.

When passersby flinch and panic at the mere sight of them, black men
can feel minimized, not only as men but as human beings. Although they
are supposedly free members of society, theirs is an edgy freedom; black
men cultivate a sense of wariness, for they are regarded warily by others.

One day I was browsing in an antique shop with a black male friend,
whom I'll call Chad. He is a calm, engaging man—anything but threatening. We strolled up and down the aisles admiring the merchandise,
then Chad headed down a narrow aisle that had no clear exit. A young
white woman in that aisle was reaching for an item on the shelf, but when
she saw Chad she jerked her arm back with fright and backed away as if
she felt cornered. Chad was distressed by her reaction—but even worse,
he felt humiliated that I had witnessed this woman reacting to him as if he
were a common criminal.

Tony, a respected businessman, experienced a similar sting. One
summer he reserved a cottage in a luxurious resort at the North Carolina
shore. As he, his wife, and their three young children drove up to the gate,
a security guard halted the van.

"Sorry, the help doesn't come in this gate. You people have to go
around to the side."

The children were shaken. One of them cried, "Do we have to go
home, Daddy?"

As he tried to contain his rage, Tony managed to pull the reservation
form out of his wallet to show the guard. The guard looked mortified as
he stuttered, "Sorry, sir . . . private property, you know. Have to be
careful who we let in."

As Tony drove through the gate, he said, "Well, kids, you've just had
your first basic lesson in Racism in America 101. I probably earn at least

four times more money than that security guard does. But because I'm black, he assumes that I'm just a hired hand."

I would bet that virtually every black man in America has such stories to tell. The insults can have a devastating cumulative effect; they are a major influence on the persona black men feel compelled to present to the world. The "mask" many black men wear is designed to reflect competence and confidence; it is supposed to keep white men and black women from witnessing how vulnerable black men often feel. Behind the mask, black men long to have their sense of self supported, nurtured, and loved. Yet black men tell me that in order to survive they feel they must work hard never to expose their soft, needy, and vulnerable interiors.

Dr. Winston Gooden, an associate professor of psychology at the Fuller Seminary School in California, believes that a man who is repeatedly treated as an object of fear and scorn can suffer from "narcissistic injury": "His ego is insulted over and over again by a society which has typed him as less than human. He experiences pain and shame at the same time. Yet to feel manly he must deny the emotional injury; he does so by internalizing the feelings and playing them out in passively aggressive or hostile behavior."

Many black men feel that their high visibility makes them convenient targets for white society's fears and hostilities. The media help to perpetuate racist attitudes by repeatedly depicting black men as endangered, dangerous, lazy, and irresponsible. Many people absorb these distortions as fact, believing that most black men are deviant and nonproductive members of society. The negativity overshadows the legions of black men who are leading full and purposeful lives.

Essence magazine's eleventh annual men's issue explored the subject of race and how white men and African-American men really feel about each other. Jon Pareles, a music critic for the *New York Times*, wrote that "white middle-class people hear [rap] music and it sounds loud and abrasive. The white interpretation is: That is an angry, young, black male person; he must be angry at me." This perceived anger makes white people anxious, Pareles explained, and their anxiety creates undue tension and a need to keep black men under control.

A nineteen-year-old black man named Malik told me in vivid terms how difficult it is for him to find himself in today's society.

"I can't remember exactly when I started to be concerned about my manhood. I think it was probably around middle school when the guys started really noticing the girls," Malik said. "I wanted to be noticed by the girls too, but there seemed to be so many issues that went along with being noticed. The guys all thought that the girls would flock to me because of my light skin and curly hair, and this made me uncomfortable. What was I supposed to do? I wanted the girls to like me, but I didn't want the fellas mad at me either. You wouldn't believe how many fights among boys are about things like hair texture and color, how tough you look and act, or what neighborhood you live in. It seems silly to grown-ups, but it is a serious matter to me because I could get shot over something stupid like this."

Malik grew up in a two-parent family in a suburban neighborhood. Yet for some reason he felt guilty about his middle-class upbringing. He tried very hard to be one of the boys, and he firmly believed that in order to fit in he had to change the way he looked and spoke, and hide the fact that his parents earned a more than adequate living. Although Malik was a very articulate young man, I noticed that he constantly switched between the vernacular of the street and the well-spoken English that was more natural for him. When I remarked about the changes in his language, he laughed. "Using the wrong tone or words in certain places or with some of the guys I know could get me into big trouble. If they heard the way I speak at home, they would call me a chump or a white boy."

Hearing Malik's story made me think about all the young black men I see who worry so much about not being seen as a wimp or less than a man. That someone as young as Malik was so overly concerned with appearing manly is a testament to the ongoing struggle of black men to find out who they are. His story also illustrates how the search for manhood affects a man's relationships with women. It is not enough to satisfy a woman's needs because a black man is also plagued with the inner voice of other black men who are always evaluating him on the masculinity scale to see how he measures up. Unfortunately, many men decide they would rather be right with "their boys" than right with their woman.

Any man—black or white—is most vulnerable when his masculine identity is threatened or uncertain. He feels he must prove to himself and to others, in every way possible, that he is a man. Perhaps most threatening of all is an intimate relationship with a woman—and nowhere do men and women clash more over power and control issues than in the black community.

Black Women: Targets, Threats, or Allies?

When a man's self-esteem is repeatedly bruised by a hostile world, surely he would want to see his woman as an oasis—someone to turn to for comfort. Unfortunately the reverse is often the case. Many of the black men I see spend an inordinate amount of their psychic energy on building elaborate defense systems to keep them safe, not just from white men but from black women as well.

Some black men transform their survival mode in the outside world into an attack mode at home. Even those who keep their anger under control are often "on alert" around black women—hardly an attitude conducive to love. They are so preoccupied with honing survival skills that they can seem hypersensitive and closed off emotionally. When black women ask me why their men can't love them the way they yearn to be loved, I ask them how black men can give love to women freely when they are in such constant struggle within themselves.

One young black woman wrote poignantly about her understanding of the black man's struggle in an issue of *Hilltop*, the student newspaper of Howard University in Washington, D.C.: "How can a man believe in you, when he cannot believe in himself? How can he lift your spirits, when he has no hopes? How can he walk with you on your road to success, if he does not know what road he would like to take? How can he give himself to you, when he does not know what he has to offer? He can't."

I wish more women showed such compassion. While black women can be very vocal about the failures of black men, I rarely hear them empathize with men's struggles. Black men are often reluctant to share their rage and unresolved pain with black women because they feel they can expect little sympathy. Instead, they are likely to hear, "Your anger sounds like a long whine. It's just another excuse for not meeting your responsibilities and performing your manly duties. I'm tired of hearing you complain about 'the system.' That's just a cop-out. After all, black women have to deal with racism, too. Why do you guys talk as if your situation is so much worse?"

Whether it is true or not, many black men *believe* that black women experience racism differently, and that some even enjoy some favored status with white men. And even though black men acknowledge that black women suffer economically just as they do, some men believe there is a crucial difference: this society judges men by their economic status, but women are supposed to obtain economic status *through* their men. Thus, they reason, men are indeed worse off. And their ever-self-reliant women just exacerbate the situation when they try to tell men how to handle and negotiate the pitfalls of a racist society. With every piece of advice women offer, men pay them right back with resentment.

Sigmund Freud observed half a century ago that men seldom live comfortably with their manhood; they are stuck with constantly having to prove it. Black men often feel that they have little control in the outside world, so they go to the opposite extreme at home and insist on total control. Yet as we discussed in chapter 2, black women are trained to be self-sufficient rulers of their own destiny. Home then becomes a battle-field for control, with men and women seeing each other as threats, not allies. Women often verbalize their control ("Don't try to tell me what to do!"), while men often distance themselves from those they care about through silence or absence, or by making caustic comments that they know will alienate their mate.

Some black men elude commitment altogether, but by the time most men reach thirty or forty they find the lack of attachment frightening. The men who sit at bars or run up and down on basketball and tennis courts on weekends are not always having as much fun as some women may think. Men who feel insecure about their maleness and about their desirability to the opposite sex often concentrate on activities that shore up their sense of themselves as men. Spending time lifting weights, jogging, or biking helps a man escape an empty apartment or even an empty relationship.

Most black men are not trained to take care of each other emotionally. They are not socialized to bond with other men except in the most superficial ways. Where women can have their treasured sessions with girlfriends and let it all hang out, most men have no such form of release. Byron, a young black man, said that black men have too much to deal with.

"On the job, you have people hassling you and after work you have women who want something from you," Byron said. "When you get together with the boys at the end of the week, they are all talking about their women. You know, like 'Man, she was really live' or she was this and that. They never say how they feel about anything. We have no common place to come to and say, 'Wow, I'm going through the same thing.' When we feel pain, we go shoot a few hoops or sweat it out in the gym. It would be helpful if we could just cry a little."

The Black Men's Roundtable: "Why the Sisters Get Me Down"

Fortunately, some men seek help, opening themselves to the rigors of counseling to avoid the loneliness that haunts them. One of the most surprising developments in my therapy practice in recent years has been the sudden increase in the number of men who come for counseling. I used to see very few black men and often heard women complain that their men "just didn't believe in telling a stranger all their business." For several reasons, men's attitudes are changing. One reason is the TV talk show phenomenon. Women would be astonished how many men watch *Oprah* and *Donahue*. Psychological terms that were once the purview of professionals are now understood by many laypeople. Several men have also told me they were influenced by the so-called men's movement, through which men join consciousness-raising groups to get in touch with the spirit and meaning of manhood. Other men are simply fed up with relationship failures and want to learn to be more sensitive and understanding with women.

To create an atmosphere of "safety" in which men could speak freely to one another without fear of judgment, a male colleague and I formed a black men's support group. The men range in age from twenty-five to forty-five, and are a mixed group professionally. They include a lawyer, a gastroenterologist, a postal clerk, the head of an investment firm, a sanitation truck driver, and several government workers. It is in these men-only sessions that I get a vivid picture of how ambivalent black men are toward black women. Following is an excerpt from a session in which the men discussed why black women "ticked them off." Wayne, a construction worker, opened up the discussion.

WAYNE: Something really upset me this weekend, and I want to talk about it. I had a long day at work when my boss comes up to me toward the end of my shift to ask if I was interested in some overtime. I jumped at the chance for the extra money, thinking in the back of my mind that maybe now I could give Anita that trip to Jamaica she keeps talking about. I'm tired of hearing about all her girlfriends who get to go to the Caribbean and all that. If I could get some extra money together, I thought I could just take her and maybe she'd be happy.

MARK: Well, aren't you a nice guy! If she wants to go to Jamaica so bad, why can't she help get the money together? How does it get to be all on you?

WAYNE: I don't mind doing things for my lady. In fact, I kind of like it. It makes me feel like the man in the family. [Room fills with laughter.] But I want to be appreciated for what I do, and that's what pisses me off with Anita. After I did my overtime, all I could think about was catching a little sleep. But when I get to our apartment, the door is bolted so I can't get in. I banged and banged, but she wouldn't answer. I couldn't believe it. When I went downstairs to a pay phone to call her, she starts yelling and screaming about where I had been all this time, and no matter what I said, she didn't believe I was at work. I probably should have called her, but I figured I could explain it all when I got home.

STEVEN: You see, that's what I always tell you guys about the sisters. You are never going to get any slack. One misunderstanding, and "bam" you're in trouble. I don't know how you all take it. I would have kicked that door in and let her know that I wasn't putting up with her shit. And I would have let her know that her precious trip to Jamaica was on its way down the tubes. Let her deal with that.

MARK: The sisters are something, man. They want, want, want. And then they expect that if they give you a little bit, you owe them. Damn, even after a one-night stand, they start making demands about what they want you to give them. It ticks me because I may not be planning to see 'em again anyway. Who do they think they are? They want to control everything, and then on top of that, they want you to take care of them. I've got news for them.

WAYNE: When I finally got Anita calmed down and convinced that I hadn't been hanging out, I could see she felt bad about locking me out. But she never said she was sorry. She just gave me a lecture about making sure that I called her the next time I had to work late. She sounded just like my mother.

Black men need women, but depending so much on them makes the men feel too much "at risk," so they put up a fight. This is why we see black men playing so many games of subterfuge and control. When they need love or an intimate connection with a black woman, they believe they must control the interaction or be dominated once again. Therefore black men have developed a style of loving that is confounding to black women. It's a style designed to control women while offering them love and commitment, a style full of anger and hostility that gets masked as macho behavior. While black men are struggling to define themselves and get respect from the white world, black women become easy targets for their feelings of inadequacy and powerlessness, in part because black men feel surrounded by women at every turn. They are raised by black women, many of their teachers are black women, many of their co-workers and even some of their supervisors are black women. At some point, I think black men say "Enough already. Give me a break from black women."

The Need for Control

Many of my male clients come to my office saying they are desperately in need of instruction on the ways and means of romance. But what they really want to know is how to love a black woman without her gaining the upper hand. Control is everything, they feel, and a relationship is a series of tactical maneuvers.

Following are some of the maneuvers men use to exert control—and how they can backfire.

If I Split My Heart in Two, You Can't Break It

Leroy, a sixty-year-old man who has been married for over forty years, often sits in on the roundtable discussions. The other guys in the group affectionately call him an "oldhead"—a voice of experience. Leroy is a colorful storyteller who enjoys regaling the younger men with tales about the travails of loving two women at once.

"I got to give my wife, Helen, a lot of credit," Leroy said one day. "Long before I was totally committed to the marriage, she was. She intended to stay married to me no matter what. And I tested her—often. I had another lady on the side, and you know I wouldn't do my stuff in public or anything, but eventually Helen found out about the other woman. What I think now is that I got a lack of attention on her part mixed up with a lack of love. I am a hugger, a toucher, a kisser. For a lot of years I asked Helen for more of all that, but she wasn't into it. Finally I took a break from the marriage—we call it my vacation. I went away, had some flings, had some fun. And then I went back home. I believe that's why we're still together today. I put Helen on notice that I wasn't going to put up with anything she put down. And she let me know that no matter what I did, she would always be there for me. Maybe I came to my senses, or maybe I just got tired out. But I'm not running around on her anymore."

Leroy's mother had unwittingly contributed to her son's turbulent marriage. She used to tell Leroy, "Always let your wife know that *you're* the man." Leroy's way of doing this was to split his emotions between his two women; by never being fully available to either one, he felt he was more available to himself, less vulnerable to a woman's power. He felt that having two women put him in the power position—"I thought I was king of the turf," he said one day. He really did love his wife, but loving was scary. If he split his heart in two by himself, he could keep his wife from breaking his heart if she ever decided she didn't love him anymore. Dividing his attentions kept his heart intact and protected. He justified this behavior to himself by faulting his wife for never being "a hugger, a toucher, a kisser"—not stopping to wonder why on earth she *should* want to hug, touch, or kiss a man who was running around on her! After years of testing his wife's love, Leroy finally allowed himself to get closer with her.

Most such stories, of course, do not have such "happy" endings. Most women demand more of their husbands than part-time love and lots of aggravation. But Helen always maintained, "I don't care where he goes or who he's with, he'll always come back to me." Like many women, she had low expectations of Leroy—or any other man. And while Leroy was seeing another woman, Helen was running her household, being in charge of her own life, which was her main goal all along.

The Best Advice: Don't Be Nice

Black men often feel that struggling to prove their competency to a woman is a no-win proposition; they are frequently genuinely perplexed when a woman doesn't see their efforts as good enough. Since many men are hypersensitive to criticism, they decide that a way to deflect it is to show a woman that they don't really value her opinion anyway. When men are nice, they figure, a woman can get close enough to hurt; if men aren't nice, she'll give them space.

Malcolm, a forty-seven-year-old client, told me that he said hurtful things to his girlfriend just to get her to back off. "I could see her hurt and I knew I was wrong, but I couldn't stop myself," he said. "My feeling was, 'You are a woman, I'm not going to let you know too much about me.' I've learned that when you provoke women, they will back off. Then I can remain at a safe distance."

Black men also often fear that they will be used if they appear too nice, or that seeming nice is a sign of weakness. At a roundtable discussion one day, several men discussed the hazards of niceness:

STEVEN: You just can't show women how you really feel. I have more success when I act like I don't care—then they're all over me. That's my whole game and believe me, it works with the sisters every time.

MARK: I've tried that game too, man. And you're right, they do fall for it. Except when you really start to care about one of 'em, it's hard to keep the "I-don't-care game" going. What gets me is that they tell you they want a man who is comfortable with his feelings, but when you try to get a little understanding by talking and revealing some deep stuff, they start looking at you funny. It's like suddenly you ain't a man no more.

WAYNE: Yeah, that's it. I try this all the time with Anita. You know, I try to be real with her. Next thing I know she's taking advantage of me, and I always believe it's because she starts thinking, "Oh, this dude is a softy, so I can work him over real good."

A prickly man, of course, runs some risks. His woman might find someone else who isn't afraid to treat her well. It feels awfully good to be appreciated; why should she stay with a man who insults her?

Another risk, of course, is that a man may find that his macho persona has become a prison he can't get out of. When he finally decides to let down his guard, the gruff mask he's been wearing for so long may seem almost impossible to take off. He longs to get close to a woman, but he discovers that he is terrified to shed the mask that has shielded him; he feels naked without it.

Therapy can help a man get rid of his mask—but only if he is really committed to the idea. Recently I saw such a man for his second therapy session.

"So how's your week been since I last saw you?" I asked.

He paused before answering and looked down at his shoes. Softly, he replied, "Well, I'll tell you. This week's been kind of rough. I kept thinking of the questions you asked me at the first session and how I kept my feelings in. Instead of really answering you, all my energy went into not letting you see how you got to me. The truth is, I kept feeling like I wanted to cry."

"Give yourself time," I replied. "Maybe when we explore what makes you feel so reluctant to trust people, you'll feel safer sharing your feelings."

You Can't Hit a Moving Target

Some men are so terrified of getting close to a woman that they construct an elaborate system for playing the field. They do a strategic dance, strictly limiting how often they will see women and for how long. Their tactics work best on naïve women who can't see through the maneuvers, and who hold out hope that if they hold on long enough, their man will come to love them only.

Charles, a forty-two-year-old single man-about-town, carefully manipulates and scripts all his relations with women to make sure he stays in control. He openly admits to me that he takes advantage of "nice girls," introducing them to sexual pleasures they have never known before.

Once they are "addicted," he pulls back. He wants to make sure they understand that *he* is in control.

AUDREY: So the ladies you see don't ask to spend weekends with you?

CHARLES: No, no one has ever pressured me for a whole weekend. That's why I say my situation is a lot different than a lot of guys I know, even though I don't associate with a lot of men. But no woman has ever pressured me.

AUDREY: Or maybe they use subtle pressure? Subtle manipulation? Is it that maybe you don't realize it's happening, when it's happening?

CHARLES: You mean them to me, or me to them?

AUDREY: Them to you.

CHARLES: No, that's what I'm saying, it's the other way around. They wait and just let it be the way it's going to be. No one has ever pressured me in any kind of way.

AUDREY: They leave it on your terms.

CHARLES: Um hum.

AUDREY: Do you like that?

CHARLES: Yes. (Laughter)

AUDREY: Why?

CHARLES: Because it makes it easier for me to do the things I have to do. Or it makes it easier for me to find the person I'm looking for, but at the same time enjoy my freedom. And that's what it's about. Being free until that time comes. That's how I feel about it. No one should be obligated to anyone until they make a commitment.

AUDREY: Do women get obligated to you? Is there a woman who decides on her own, without your pressure, to be exclusive? With the hope that . . .

CHARLES: Well, they all seem to be that way.

AUDREY: So they are all seeing you exclusively?

CHARLES: They all seem to be like that. I don't know for a fact, I mean, I wouldn't swear to it. But it appears that way. Most of the time when I call they are there. I don't date many women all at one time. It used to be maybe one, two, or three. But they all seem to be pretty available.

AUDREY: But career women travel, and belong to ski clubs and tennis clubs.

CHARLES: Most of the ones that I have dated recently were free most of the time. It seems like they all just did their job and did the meetings periodically and then were home. They went to a few functions here or there, but like I say, I don't question their whereabouts. I don't question them because I don't want them to question me.

I have a very controlled situation in all my relationships. One thing I know about anything that you do, if you kind of take charge of it from the beginning and run it, it will go that way. When you let a woman believe she can see you whenever she wants, that's when you get in trouble.

AUDREY: I see.

CHARLES: I always let it be known upfront that I'm very busy and that I don't have a lot of time. So they don't expect a lot, they don't look for a lot. And even if they get sexually addicted, they don't come pawing and begging and stuff, because it just ain't going to work. I back them up in my own kind of way. Not nasty or anything, it's just . . .

AUDREY: How do you back them up?

CHARLES: Well, if I plan a nice evening and we end up coming back to my place, I make it clear that the next morning I've got a lot of work to do and we will have to break early in the day.

AUDREY: I know of a lot of women who won't leave when it's time.

CHARLES: Oh, they're gone. They are out of there.

AUDREY: How do you get them to leave? I knew a guy who arranged to have a friend phone him so he could pretend that he had an emergency. This was so he could get the woman out of his house when he was ready.

CHARLES: Well, if necessary I will leave even if it's just to go around the corner. I get up, I get dressed, and I leave. So most of the time they don't want to stay there after I've gone.

AUDREY: Oh, really? Because some women will tell you they'll stay until you return.

CHARLES: No, they don't do that. I don't know why. I think it's just the way that it goes down from the beginning. I just say to them: "See, I have an alarm system. I don't want the house to be without an alarm. So if you leave after I'm gone, the house is not alarmed. I would prefer that you leave with me."

AUDREY: Do they know that when they come?

CHARLES: They know that when they come, yeah.

Anyone who has such a strong need to be in control feels deeply *out* of control inside. It takes a pretty frightened guy to go through all those antics. Charles would deny that, of course. He defined masculinity as the ability to control women. So by his measure, he was on top of the game, a master planner. He even felt that at some level, he was really being honest with these women. He certainly laid down the law from the beginning, informing them that he was not often available. Some women, of course, are so desperate to believe that they can make such a man "see the light" that they will tolerate his manipulations and the rations of time that he grants them. They know not to test him because he will run. So Charles and men like him keep women where they want them: hanging in the wind, waiting by the phone.

I Give You Everything Else: Don't Ask for My Heart, Too

Some men see love as a system of emotional bartering. It goes something like this: "If I take care of you, surely you will take care of me." The problem is that what some men believe constitutes "taking care of" a woman may be very different from what women say they want. I know men who will go to great lengths to explain all that they are doing for a woman—but they almost never mention anything about her emotional needs. They might say, "Yes, I am away from home a lot, but she has a roof over her head, food in the refrigerator, and a car in the driveway. And every now and then, I even buy a gift or two. So what does she want from me?" He can provide a ready list of his generous actions: he fixed her refrigerator, took her car to the shop, picked up Chinese food for dinner, took the kids to the playground while she got her hair done. In his mind, he is "taking care of business," as black men love to say. But the emotional exchange women long for is totally lacking.

The dynamic is reminiscent of the "custodial care" and "conditional love" types of parenting described in chapter 3. For some men, providing food, clothing, shelter, or a dozen roses enables them to perpetuate the fiction that the women are dependent on them—and that they are independent of the women. The best love relationships, of course, are *interdependent*, free of the list making that "proves" who gives more. Through emotional bartering men protect themselves from what they most fear: a woman's anger and disappointment, which in turn could ultimately lead her to abandon and reject her man. Some men feel deeply defensive of their true dependence on women. They are aware that women give life, that only through women can men become fathers, that men need women profoundly. But such dependence makes them feel precarious. So they cling to the image of needing nothing: "I can take care of myself. I don't really need her all that much." Although he feeds himself this line repeatedly, he never completely swallows it. Deep down, he knows he would feel lost without his woman.

I remember once being ten minutes late for an appointment with a male client who was anxiously waiting for me in the office vestibule. When I came through the door and apologized, he looked incredibly relieved. He said that he had become very nervous and uncertain if he should wait. "I thought you had left me," he said. I explored with him in the session what my lateness represented for him. He said that he remembered many times depending upon his mother to pick him up after he finished school, but she was often late. "I remember many times feeling forgotten by my mother, who was always doing something for someone else. I remember longing for her to notice that I had needs too," he said. This fear of abandonment manifested itself in his present fear of closeness with the women in his life. He couldn't let any woman get too close because he could never feel confident that she wouldn't leave or abandon him.

Some men's feeling that they must barter for love stems from never having been unconditionally loved as children. Instead, as discussed in chapter 3, they were raised to believe that they were worthy of love only if they met certain conditions, such as behaving well, getting good grades, and doing chores. Conditionally loved children often become adults who believe that no one can love them just for themselves. Some men wear themselves out trying to show their mates that they are doing all they can to provide for the family—when what their families really need is time together and communication.

A Woman Needs to Know Her Place

In her book *Possessing the Secret of Joy*, Alice Walker theorizes that one reason some African societies perform clitoridectomies—a form of genital mutilation—on their women is to prevent them from leaving their husbands to pursue the joys of female sexuality. Walker refers to female genital mutilation as an act of "clipping her wings." Of course, other cultures, too, devise ways of clipping women's wings; for example, they pay them less for their work, pass laws that favor men, or mock aggressive, successful women for not being "feminine" enough.

Individual men, too, find ways to clip their partners' wings. Consider, for example, the married man who does not help out much around the house because he wants to make sure his wife has so much to do that she couldn't begin to think about going anywhere. Or the single man who devises games of high drama just to keep a woman off-balance and enthralled. He reasons that if she never knows exactly where she stands, she will work even harder, in her state of constant longing, to win his heart. He feels safe leaving her in this precarious position because he believes she will keep coming after him for more, and he won't have to worry about her going off with someone else.

One man, Daniel, clipped his wife's wings by "taking wing" himself whenever she displeased him. He pulled a disappearing act when they argued, staying away for days at a time.

"It drives me crazy when he stalks out of the house and doesn't show up or call for days," said his wife, Catherine. "He could be lying in a ditch somewhere or with another woman. I have no idea what he's up to and I think it's so unfair, because when he comes back the thing that drove him away is still not solved. I'm afraid to get into a disagreement with him because he'll threaten to leave if he doesn't get his way."

The irony was that although Daniel wanted Catherine to believe that he went to another woman when he disappeared, the truth was that he was usually alone. "Sometimes I just check into a hotel for a few days until she comes to her senses," he said. "When she acts crazy I need an escape hatch and that's why I leave." His actions made her feel insecure, which was just what he wanted. By vanishing or threatening to do so, he got her to do what he wanted when he wanted it.

And then there's the man who feigned illness each time his wife expressed displeasure with him. These illnesses would take him to his bed, so naturally he could not address her concerns because he claimed to be too sick to deal with her. This cycle also set her up to be the "heavy" in the relationship. How could she attack a sick man and not feel guilty? In any event, she was now too busy taking care of him to think of pursuing an argument.

Such control maneuvers are the flip side of fear. Just as white men have sought to suppress black men because they have feared black men's power, so do many black men fear and try to suppress black women's power, especially the power of their rage.

Many black men never shake their dread of feminine anger; many even find it immobilizing. It often takes them back to a childhood when a mother, grandmother, or teacher was unhappy with them and expressed her anger in a stern and hostile manner. With so many female authority figures in their lives, black boys grow up wanting total freedom from women. In my office, I've heard women yelling and screaming at grown men and watched them withdraw and retreat right in the sessions. A friend of mine once described to me his experience after a turbulent encounter with a girlfriend. He went home and climbed into his bed, imagining himself the size of a one-year-old. He fell asleep and began dreaming about this hulklike creature who changed size right before his eyes. She seemed like an Amazon. He felt his heart pounding, and a rush of nausea overtook him as he tried to flee to safety. He awoke shaking and sweating. Intellectually he knew that she couldn't harm him, but nothing in his psyche could assure him of that. His dream exemplifies how many men feel when they are confronted head-on with a woman's rage.

Many men also tell me they have great difficulty witnessing a woman's pain, especially if they feel they may have caused it. Men have an innate need to be the problem solver, a role that shores up their feeling of being in control.

When a woman is crying, a man often feels helpless. He wants to figure out, in exact measure, what will soothe her pain. If he cannot comfort her, his own sense of powerlessness becomes overwhelming and he will become distant or leave the scene entirely. His actions may give her the impression that he doesn't care, and leave her more distraught than ever. Yet he is probably somewhere ruminating about his inadequacies because he had failed to understand or cope with his woman's anguish.

Musical Chairs

A handsome forty-two-year-old black businessman named Van, who had never been married, related the highlights of his romantic life to me with great pride. Lots of women chased him, while he sat back and decided which ones he would see and when he would see them. He had decided that many socially sheltered black women, no matter how successful professionally, felt unsure of themselves with men. This made them prime targets for his "loving" advances.

Van needed women to bolster his confidence in his masculinity, and believed that having many women was a reassuring sign of his drawing power. To be respected as a real black man, he felt he had to move many different women in and out of his life. Van liked to think of himself as another Wilt Chamberlain, the basketball star who claimed in his autobiography to have slept with more than twenty thousand women throughout his career.

"I like pretty much having my way. The women seem to need me," Van said. "One woman wrote me a long loving letter once about how much she cared for me and wanted a commitment. The letter was powerful and made me feel real good. But I couldn't bring myself to ever mention how it affected me. Believe it or not, we never really discussed it. It was almost like I never received it. She didn't say anything and neither did I. I couldn't believe she continued to see me, even though I ignored her letter."

Van had designed a "social program" that women found very attractive: he sent flowers, planned romantic evenings, and treated them to exotic trips. He prided himself on his ability to liberate women from old, restrictive sexual patterns. He especially enjoyed turning "nice ladies" on to innovative sexual practices as a way to keep them hooked on him, and let them think they might have a future with him by dropping hints about "settling down when I find the right woman."

"When a woman insists that I make a commitment, sometimes I'll intensify discussions about a potential engagement, offer her a ring, or even take her on trips to look at houses." Incredibly, Van felt no guilt about deceiving these women because, he said, "I'm just giving them what they want to hear."

Van's father was a moody, impulsive man who terrorized his wife and children with hostile accusations and verbally abusive comments. To avoid identifying with his mother and feeling like a victim, Van became a controller like his father, but created a different look for the same behavior. He coped with the negative identification with his father by internalizing an ideal view of himself; he frequently described himself as "a nice, giving, and compassionate guy." To use a term coined by Anna Freud, Van identified with the aggressor, meaning that he incorporated his father's threatening behaviors as a way of coping with anxiety and insults to the ego. Yet when I suggested that perhaps his pattern with women was directly linked to how his parents related, Van balked. He didn't want to see the connection.

"I don't put restrictions on people," Van said. "Women come after me because they like what I do and say. I don't beg anyone to stay with me." Van refused to recognize that he was a controlling, self-centered, manipulative man who structured relationships with women to support his shaky ego. It never occurred to him that his partners might suffer—as he and his siblings and mother had suffered years before.

A Backup Woman for Security

Men often have affairs to shield against intimacy and retain control of their relationship. Having a backup woman can make men feel protected, since they do not trust that any one woman will be there when they need her. Because black men have such a great need to feel safe, they often seek comfort in the arms of the many willing partners they can find. An affair is also an ego boost and a prop for sagging self-esteem.

Kevin was a single, divorced stockbroker who believed that having multiple partners would help him affirm himself. He came to my office for therapy after noticing that he was having difficulty making an emotional connection with Sheila, a woman he had been dating for a year. He thought he might really care about her, but something was stopping him from going forward.

KEVIN: What do women want? I make good money, and I don't mind spending it. If I have several women, what difference does it make as long as I treat them all well?

AUDREY: Why do you think you need to have several women?

KEVIN: I'm crazy about Sheila. She's the one I see the most, and to be honest it is getting harder to juggle the others. I don't have time, though, for a lot of demands. You know: "Where are you going? What time will you be home? Who is that woman I saw you with?" It always comes down to this kind of stuff, and I'm not up to it. I feel safer when I have a couple of other women waiting in the wings.

AUDREY: You mean you have difficulty coping with the unknown.

KEVIN: I have a strong need to be in control. My father said a man who can't control a woman is out of control.

AUDREY: Do you agree with that statement?

KEVIN: I guess I must. When I was in high school, I was dumped by a couple of chicks. I wanted one so much. She left me for a guy who ran track. You know—a big star. I have had several experiences like that with women.

AUDREY: I'm sure that left you feeling real bad.

KEVIN: Yes it did. My ego was crushed for quite a while.

AUDREY: Have you ever tried to relate to only one woman?

KEVIN: I've tried a few times. I can do the social part. I can handle the sexual part. But when something heavy starts, I get scared.

AUDREY: What scares you the most?

KEVIN: Suppose I give my all to one woman and she decides that I'm not what she really wants. That's an awful feeling for a man. It's like this chick has you by the nose and all your buddies are teasing you, but you're so happy you don't care. Then she dumps you, and you feel like a chump, not just to yourself but to your friends as well. I don't want to feel like that.

AUDREY: You seem very concerned about a woman leaving you. Why is that?

KEVIN: Because I know how these women are. One day they're with you, the next day they aren't. They are always looking for something better. So I do the same thing. I've always got my eyes open to something else, just in case things don't work out.

Kevin's history set him up for this emotional conflict because he had no idea of what intimacy is or looks like when displayed between a man and woman. He couldn't remember ever seeing his parents demonstrate intimate feelings. His parents exchanged no kisses, hugs, or terms of endearment. He assumed his parents loved each other because his father gave orders and his mother carried them out. Kevin followed orders, too. He always did what he was told—and never expressed how he felt or what he wanted because no one ever asked him. His father was stoic and never showed emotion; he regarded such displays as weakness and demanded that his son behave as he did.

Now having multiple partners was Kevin's way of feeling powerful and reducing his fears of dependency. He wanted an intimate relationship with Sheila, but felt too scared and vulnerable to tell her. He feared that if he got too close with Sheila, he might lose himself.

Kevin, like many black men, had a fear of engulfment so overpowering that he would do almost anything to avoid feeling vulnerable to the whim of another, especially when that other is a black woman. Men often fantasize engulfment as women's attempt to overwhelm them and overpower them. In many cases this fantasy stems from young boys' earlier experience of feeling "swallowed up" by a mother's power to give or withhold emotional or physical nurturance.

Yet by running from intimacy, men actually deny themselves what they want most. Although many women assume that a man avoiding commitment does not want to relate intimately, the truth is that he often doesn't know how to attach or feel intimacy and protect his masculinity at the same time. He has not yet discovered that love, rather than tying him down and making him feel dominated, can set him free.

Some Would Rather Switch Than Fight

Many black men decide at some point during their social development that black women are too stressful to deal with, so they switch to women of other ethnic groups. One of the largest crossover relationships in America is marriages between black men and white women. According to the U.S. Census Bureau, in 1992 there were 157,000 interracial couples in which the husband was black and the wife was white. Almost 4 percent of black men are married to women who are not black. Interracial dating increased during the sixties, when sexual mores and strictures became more relaxed. The opening up of biracial dating was mainly between black men and white women, not between white men and black women (although this pattern now seems to be on an upward swing).

In exploring "the man thing," one has to consider how power, entitlement, and gender reinforcement tie directly into cross-cultural dating and marriages.

Black men often fantasize that loving white women—or women from some other group—will be less stressful and more fulfilling. Few black men don't wonder at least once or twice about how much different and better an interracial arrangement might be.

Men give various motivations for relating to white women. More often than not, I hear black men say that white women are more supportive, less competitive with them, easier to get along with. They also say that white women are more liberated sexually than black women. In fact, it is almost impossible to talk about interracial dating without talking about sex and sexual stereotypes. Some black men buy into the stereotype of white women as subservient women who are constantly available, both sexually and otherwise; in contrast, the stereotype of black women is that they give men more hassles and are more uptight sexually. While stereotypes, by definition, are specious, they are tenacious, too. When many people see an interracial couple, they make assumptions about what attracted them to each other, and about their life in the bedroom.

Competition with white males is a powerful component of black men dating and marrying white women, although few black men would admit this. I believe it's a way some black men feel they can get back at white men, a way to get even with the men they blame for their lowered status in this country. Some black men even see having a white woman as the ultimate display of success, a notion that drives some black women crazy.

Best-selling author Bebe Moore Campbell expressed the black woman's outrage about interracial dating in an article in the *New York Times*: "Regardless of the statement black men with white women want to make, or even if they wish to make one, what many black women receive is a hurtful mixture of blatant sexism and eerie internecine racism: If you were good enough (if you looked like white women and didn't give me so much back talk), I wouldn't choose someone else. The message that they don't measure up makes some sisters want to scream."

Black men who decide to relate outside of the race don't seem particularly bothered by black women's negative reaction. A male caller to my radio show said, "The white woman I'm dating is so reasonable and she puts no pressure on me. She understands when I don't have any money and will share what she has with me. The sisters want, want, want, and I'm sick of them." Some men admit they are tired of being lonely and very tired of the harassment from black women, so they settle down with women of other ethnic groups.

When black football star O. J. Simpson was charged with murdering his white wife, Nicole, and a friend of hers, the race issue came up time and again. Some polls showed that many blacks identified with him, and felt O. J. could not get a fair trial because he was black. Eleanor Holmes Norton, the District of Columbia delegate to Congress, told *Time* magazine, "For many blacks, every black man is on trial. O. J. Simpson has become the proxy not because the black man is a criminal but because the black man is increasingly seen as a criminal by virtue of his sex and color."

Yet other black people did not identify with O. J. They felt that through his lavish lifestyle and marriage to a white woman he had disconnected himself from the black community. Conrad Worrill, chairman of the National Black United Front in Chicago, told *Time*, "Simpson did not function within our race. His wife, lawyers, and housekeepers were white."

In TV and radio talk shows, at parties, and over dinner tables, debate was fierce: Did O. J. betray his race by marrying a white woman? Did O. J. and Nicole marry because of the sexual attraction of opposite races?

Yet as I learned more about O. J. and Nicole's backgrounds, it occurred to me that they were probably more attracted by their similarities than by their racial differences. Both had a low self-image and both coveted a glamorous lifestyle. His childhood of shame—due to being teased about a leg deformity and tattered clothes—dovetailed with her feelings of inadequacy about never having any formal education after high school. If anything, the two were overidentified with each other, clinging together on their upwardly mobile path, both fundamentally insecure. She became his identity as much as he became hers, a fusion that ultimately led to their explosive fights, repeated breakups, and inability to sustain an intact family for their children.

Despite the dynamics at play in interracial relationships, most interracial couples do not intentionally set out to find someone of another race, but happen to meet their partner through working together, living in the same apartment building, belonging to the same gym, and other casual encounters. Usually they are drawn to each other because of personal traits that may have little to do with race. And their conflicts, too, often are the same ones faced by same-race couples, despite the widely held belief that relating across color and ethnic lines somehow helps one escape the traditional pitfalls of romance.

Gus and Carol Ann, a black man and a white woman who met at college and married several years after graduation, illustrate this dynamic. Carol Ann, now in her mid-thirties, believed that their relationship had lost much of its excitement and passion. Gus had been an activist and a "big man on campus," and she had felt proud that he had chosen her to be at his side. Those were heady days, and the fact that he was willing to take the risk to be with her made her sense of self zoom through the roof.

"He was so warm and caring," she said. "I couldn't resist him. We dated secretly for about a year when he finally decided that it was time I met some of his friends. He took me to a party in a black neighborhood, and we decided I should ride there with my head down in the seat. There was no point in provoking the neighborhood folks. What I remember most about the party was the black women's angry, hostile looks and whispering. They made me uneasy, and I wasn't sure what they were reacting to or what they might do."

Gus remembered the party well, too. He said that by going to the party, Carol Ann proved how willing she was to put herself on the line for him.

"I thought, boy, if she is willing to make all these sacrifices to be with me, she will probably do the same for me when she becomes my wife." But after they got married, Gus started noticing that Carol Ann had needs of her own; while she was willing to do anything for him she also had high expectations of what he should do for her. He hadn't counted on this.

"Now whatever I do for her is never enough," he said. "She actually whines, and this drives me up a wall. Here's this courageous woman that I married reduced to whimpering and nagging about every little thing."

Interracial dating is a viable option for many men and women, but it can work only when the individuals go into it for the right reasons. Expecting an interracial romance to be one of life's great panaceas is a mistake. Couples who believe this are ultimately disappointed when they find themselves facing the same issues they would have faced with someone of the same race. Carol Ann and Gus had both expected—and felt entitled to—a lifetime of acts of bravery as they took a united stand against the common enemy of racism. Yet marriage is a daily test not of society's values but of each partner's ability to communicate, to have realistic expectations, and to work together to achieve a balanced give-and-take.

Getting His Act Together

One of the most gratifying aspects of my practice is to see a client who has worked tremendously hard to overcome great difficulties arrive at a place where both of us see such improvement that we decide that counseling is no longer necessary, at least not on a continuous basis. This, of course, does not mean that his work is finished, but that he has acquired some of the necessary tools to help him get on with his life in a healthy manner. The men who arrive at this point are often so overwhelmed with their new sense of themselves that they are often brought to tears.

Jamal and I had worked together for several years. He wanted desperately to save his marriage of nine years to Tammy, who had been his childhood sweetheart. He came in for counseling because he feared that he was forcing his wife away from him with his constant insecurities about his precarious professional life as a musician and her flourishing career as an engineer. The arguments had become so hostile that he knew he had to get some help or he was going to lose her.

"Every time we went out with her friends we would have a fight when we got home," he related to me in an early session. "I always felt that her friends were judging me or criticizing me because I didn't make as much money as she did. It made me crazy, and I would start picking at her on the way home. I guess I did this because I felt so bad myself. Eventually I refused to go to any work parties with her, and this made her furious."

Jamal wanted Tammy constantly to make amends to him because his career as a musician was not on track. If he didn't get a job after an audition, and she called and said she had to work late, he saw her as not being supportive. When she tried to talk to him about his day once she came home, he refused to discuss it and might not speak to her for days on end. She would then accuse him of being childish, which he interpreted to mean that he was "less than a man."

In our sessions, we worked on Jamal's issue of feeling entitled to Tammy's attention no matter what was going on in her own life. He began to see the connection between this feeling and how he had felt as the pampered only son of a single mother. Once he saw that he was unconsciously setting up Tammy to be another doting mom, he was willing to try some other methods to get Tammy's attention. Instead of concocting issues to fight with her about, he tried to understand what she was coping with as she tried to survive in a big company as the only black female engineer.

"One evening I decided to make dinner for her," he said. "Can you believe that I had never done this for her? I always wanted her to cook for me; I felt this would show how much I meant to her. The fact that she was often exhausted had escaped me because I was so caught up in myself. The evening I cooked, the meal wasn't that great, but you should have seen the look on her face. I couldn't believe what a great time we had that night. She listened to me for hours about the music business and how tough it is to make it in the music world. I couldn't believe how selfish I had been all of this time, making demands but not giving up much."

Making dinner for Tammy was a small gesture for Jamal, but it represented a great deal of growth. There was a time when something as simple as making dinner would have become a big issue for him, all caught up and confused with his ideas about what a woman should do for her husband. Once he was able to focus on shoring up his own fragile sense of masculinity, he was able to let many of the little things go. Battles about what was man's work and what was woman's work seemed to lessen as he worked on his own insecurities. When he realized that everything could not be his way if their relationship was going to work, he was able to accept what Tammy realistically had to offer him—not what he could force her to give.

Jamal did much of his work in a male-female support group, which helped him to understand more about how women feel and react to certain things. He was genuinely surprised by some of the discussions with the women in the group because he had not often allowed himself to really listen to what women have to say. He was often so focused on himself that he could not take in another point of view. Jamal soon learned that love was not about filling a gap, and to discover this he had to abandon his harsh demands of his wife, and become brutally honest with himself.

5

Damned If She Does, Damned If She Doesn't

"Lawd, these things we women
Have to stand!
I wonder is there nowhere a
Do-right man?"

—LANGSTON HUGHES,
Early Evening Quarrel

On a business trip to San Francisco last year, I stopped at Nordstrom's cafe for a bite to eat. While waiting for my order, I heard an irate voice and turned in the direction of the commotion. An attractive, well-dressed black woman was going ballistic with the clerk who was taking her order. She felt slighted because he had asked her to carry her own tray to the table, but had not asked white customers in front of her to carry theirs. The clerk explained that since she had ordered only a cup of tea, she could easily carry the tray herself.

"I know my rights. I know how most people are treated in here," she screamed. A waiter quickly came over and carried her tray to a table to keep her happy. Five minutes later two white women came into the restaurant and ordered coffee. The clerk asked them to carry their own trays. The black woman looked at me in total embarrassment. I felt terrible for her because I could see that she wanted some sign of moral support from me—another black woman. I felt like saying, "What's wrong? It's obvious that you are troubled." Not wanting to be intrusive, I simply smiled at her and said nothing.

But I knew instinctively that it was not the lack of service that upset this woman so much. I wondered what was going on in her life that this trivial incident could get so completely blown out of proportion. The therapist in me wanted to know with whom was this woman really angry—her boss, her child, her lover? What was making her so enraged that her anger built up and erupted at the merest hint of unfair treatment? My guess was that like many black women, she felt so chronically overwhelmed and taken advantage of that her psychological defense systems were in overdrive. She was probably thinking, "Damn, I can't even get someone to serve me a cup a tea without there being some commotion." She probably yearned for someone, somewhere (even in a Nordstrom's), to know what she needed and to offer it without her always having to ask.

Most of the black women I know feel so burdened, it's a wonder that they don't scream more often! Many live in constant motion, juggling their responsibilities as wage-earners, wives, mothers, sisters, daughters, granddaughters, nieces, lovers, friends, neighbors, churchgoers, and community members. There's little "down time" in such a life. Many women are so worn out they desperately need a break, but so pro- grammed to be on the run that they can hardly conceive of taking time out for themselves.

When I once suggested to Roberta, a very overwhelmed client, that she reserve next Saturday morning for a leisurely stroll in the park, she stared at me as if I had just proposed a jaunt to the moon. She started to recite her lengthy to-do list: "Take the kids for back-to-school clothes, pick up dry cleaning, fill out the paperwork for Mom's home-care worker, visit Granddad in the nursing home, wash the kitchen curtains, shop for groceries . . ."

". . . and save the world, all on Saturday," I interjected. Roberta started to laugh.

"You have left yourself off that list for too long," I went on. "Don't you think it's time to pencil yourself in?"

"Yes, but . . ."

"Roberta, you can't tell me you have the energy for all that without taking some time out to recharge your batteries. You deserve some time out once in a while."

I was delighted when Roberta reported at our next session that although she couldn't quite justify taking an entire morning for herself, for the first time in years she had spent an entire hour soaking in a hot bubble bath. It was a start.

But by the next week, Roberta was frazzled again—back with the program of trying to do it all, alone and with no relief in sight.

Most black women are exhausted—too competent for their own good. They are take-care-of-everything, take-care-of-everyone women, and most of the time they feel deeply unappreciated. As children, they were raised to be self-reliant: "The world is tough, honey, you have to take charge of things yourself and not depend on anybody—especially a man." As adults, they must be content with distorted and burdensome notions about women's roles and men's excuses: whether the black community rises or falls is attributed to how well women handle things. It's women's job to raise the kids and impart strong values, but men have the option to help out or not. Women should reassure and coddle their men and certainly shouldn't add to men's troubles because, after all, black men have it hard in this society. Women will do okay and take care of themselves; it's black *men* the community has to worry about.

No wonder black women are fed up! No wonder many women seem to have an "attitude" or, as some men put it, a chip on their shoulder that they dare anyone to knock off. If black women often appear ready to do battle, it's because they are constantly fighting to keep up with the inequitable expectations that have been heaped on them for too long. The most frustrating notion of all is that black women have it so much easier than black men. Society, the media, the community—all seem to focus on how men have it so rough: educationally, economically, socially, black men have to struggle. Well, yes, they do, and that's unfair. But for too long, the struggle of black women has gone largely ignored, unexplored, and unexplained. Black men often dismiss black women's troubles as being secondary to their own, and discredit women's ceaseless attempts to cope with what life has brought them.

Women are often so good at coping, they make it look easy. Yet no matter how confident and independent they may appear, in private they yearn to be appreciated, respected, and taken care of, especially by the men in their lives. Their public face of self-sufficiency and their private face of loneliness remind me of a doll I had when I was a little girl. On one side the doll had a happy face, but if you flipped her over, she had a sad face. Black women feel that they must project a self-reliant, "nothing bothers me" image to the world, but their insouciant persona is in sharp conflict with their inner wish for someone to depend on.

In a poignant essay in the *Washington Post* entitled "What About the Sisters?" Donna Britt wrote:

Who's worried about the mounting number of black women raising their kids alone; and those getting the life knocked out of them by angry, frustrated brothers? Who supports career women, whose difficulties with being black and female in an often-hostile work world are denigrated by certain black men—who suggest each sister's success is bought at a brother's expense? How about the myriad guys who suggest that while racism is real, sexism is a frivolous, white-girl notion?

Many black women can't even turn to their families for the affirmation and support they need. After all, since they were little girls they've been trained to be self-sufficient. Now that they are, their parents don't think it's all that remarkable; black women have always been the mainstay of their families and communities, haven't they? But if black *men* are self-sufficient and responsible—now *that's* something to celebrate.

In a group discussion at a conference on the black family in Nashville, Tennessee, Blaine, a thirty-six-year-old social worker, suddenly blurted out, "Black men make me sick! I can't stand hearing them complain all the time about their plight. What about mine? My mother brought me up to take care of myself no matter what. I do it and do it well. But she and my dad still baby my grown brother, Ralph, because they feel he has gotten a raw deal from white America. I have no time for this!"

Blaine seethed with resentment. "Ralph is constantly out of work or waiting for some big career deal to go through. In the meantime, my parents dole out money to him and make excuses for his behavior. My brother and I had the same upbringing, the same privileges. But my parents expect me to achieve and take care of myself while he lies around the house and goes on about what the world owes him."

Many of the women in our group nodded in sympathy with Blaine. But some of the men stirred with discomfort. Blaine's anger was surely justified, yet black women are often criticized when they speak out. They are blamed for having "sharp tongues," for having that famous "attitude."

In fact, however, black women don't speak out nearly enough about what really bothers them. Although they may vent their frustration from time to time, many find it hard to admit that they need help. Karen, a twenty-eight-year-old black woman, told me after a seminar I conducted entitled "The Superwoman Syndrome" that she was tired of always feeling that she had to be so understanding and strong. She noticed that at her job white women who complained about their heavy workloads often asked for—and received—help and support from their supervisors. But Karen felt compelled to maintain an aura of strength and toughness, as if she didn't have the right to admit that "Can-do Karen" sometimes simply *couldn't* do it all.

"Superwoman" is a myth, a surreal ideal that no human can live up to. Yet something strange happens when women expect that they can do everything: they begin to believe it. They continually swallow their frustration and push forward no matter how bone-weary they feel. Many black professional women are in conflict with their need to be dependent and their social training that implied that they should not desire it. They were taught by their parents that once they were financially independent they should be able to fully take care of themselves. Guilt comes easily for these black women because they have achieved and accumulated—professionally and materially—all that their parents and/or grandparents could have wished for. Instead of feeling fulfilled, they are fearful, depressed, and—above all—lonely, unappreciated, and unloved. Many of these women are stressed out, but feel so indispensable in their public and private worlds that they can't imagine breaking the cycle and trying out a new role. Stress even causes many of them to compromise their own well-being; they neglect their health, fail to get regular checkups, eat poorly, and rarely get the rest and exercise they need.

Reaching for a Dream

If women at least took pleasure in what they achieved professionally, materially, and personally, then maybe their ceaseless labor would make more sense. But the bargain they have bought into has not panned out.

They were taught that if they did everything they were supposed to do—get a good education, prepare for a high-paying job, and learn how to manage their personal lives independently—that the world would reward them with what they were led to believe is the good life. Black women continually tell me details about their houses, cars, clothes, and vacations. These ostensible symbols of success are extremely important to them because attaining these things allows them to feel that they have something to show for all their hard work. Yet economic achievement cannot make up for a lack of emotional nurturance.

I believe that many black women have assimilated white America's model for women: obtain an education, pursue a career, marry an equally educated and productive man, rear children, enjoy the fruits and intimacies of a materialistic and pleasure-seeking society. While many black women have indeed achieved the first two goals, they are struggling to seize the rest. Because many black men are unable to provide women with this idyllic lifestyle, black women often feel cheated out of what they think their white sisters take for granted.

The pursuit of this unrealistic dream is particularly painful for black women who are very high achievers. They believe that the man beside them should be of equal status, but unfortunately few black men can fill the bill. The women believe they have only three choices: see only black men and be willing to compromise on status and money; date men of other ethnic backgrounds who may be better able to provide the economic success they so desire; or opt to go it alone.

Going it alone is indeed what many black women are doing; some out of choice, others by default. The *Washington Post*, in a front-page story, declared that 25 percent of black women will never marry. Demographers made this estimate based on current marriage rates and historical behavior patterns. Researchers maintained that these patterns were attributable to the poor economic and social status of young black men and to the fact that black women outnumber black men. The article quoted sociologist Joyce Ladner: "The combined factors of joblessness, low skill levels, a lack of education, the social problems of substance abuse, alcoholism, imprisonment, all lead to reducing the pool of individuals who would be able to earn a living and support a family."

Many black women resent that statistics about a reduced pool of marriageable men are hammered into their heads by the media, family, and friends. Even when women find a man, they cannot escape the "man shortage" mystique that black men have choices and women don't. Carleen, a single black woman, stomped into a women's support group one evening in a state of profound disgust.

"You know what a man said to me last night? He looked me straight in the eye and said, 'Gosh, I got all these babes throwing themselves at me, why should I settle for just one, even though I really like you?' "

Another woman chimed in, "Yeah, all these men are like precious commodities. I was furious the other day when my girlfriend met my boyfriend and said to me, 'You're so lucky you found him.' Lucky? Why am I lucky? Why doesn't anyone say he's lucky to have found *me*?"

Competition for females is a game that men of all races play; for black men, it's often a power game to see who can attract not only the most women but the most beautiful, the youngest, the smartest. Acquiring many women helps some black men feel in control and powerful. Maybe they can't be a corporate tycoon, but they can still be sought-after sexual and social companions. The shortage of available black men has made some men especially cocky, like rare prizes, and made some black women feel pressured to "prove" that they deserve to win. They become consumed with manhunting, careening between hope and frustration. When they get lonely, depressed, or humiliated by their fruitless search for a mate, they often manifest passive anger in the form of withdrawal, overeating, excessive shopping, or workaholism.

Some women try to "beat the game" by proving that they aren't just "one of the pack." Their approach reminds me of the advice strippers offer in the musical *Gypsy*. "You gotta have a gimmick"—something that sets you apart, that will make you irresistible to men. Women who are intent on conquering the man shortage take on, like chameleons, whatever personality, appearance, or talent they believe will give them a competitive edge. Some women become gourmet cooks—and will cook anything a man wants, anytime he wants it. Some women try a different route to men's hearts; they cultivate sexual talents, or fashion themselves into exotic creatures well toned from obsessive dieting and sessions at the gym. I've known women to lend men money, babysit for their children, buy them expensive gifts, co-sign the lease on their apartments or cars, pick up all the expenses for luxurious vacations, let them live with them rent-free, and otherwise attempt to make themselves appealing and indispensable. I hurt for women who do all these things for external reasons—who feel that just being themselves will never be enough. Furthermore, any men who are intent on using the man shortage to their advantage are quite able to resist any woman, no matter how captivating her "gimmick."

Obsessing about finding a man is debilitating because it keeps women focused on the wrong issues. What they need to focus on is how to take better care of themselves, ask for support from others, and make better choices about the men in their lives.

What Women Do for Love

At a book-signing party in Oxon Hill, Maryland, a black man asked bestselling novelist Terry McMillan why the male characters in her books are so negative and the female characters are so angry with black men.

"For four hundred years we have been taking care of you and working ourselves to the bone trying to please you," McMillan said. "But we are tired now. We want someone to recognize us—to recognize how important we are to our communities. We want to be loved and taken care of. We want to be pleased. We want you to love us."

McMillan articulated the dream. But many women are so desperate for love that they forgo the dream and settle for men who mistreat, bore, or frustrate them. Some figure that any man is better than no man at all. Some believe that no men are particularly supportive, so any man will do. And some feel foolish for even imagining that their dream of a loving, intimate relationship is a real possibility. Devoid of much hope for anything better, many women perpetuate poor relationships by taking on a variety of self-defeating roles.

The Sapphire Complex

The image of a domineering, controlling, and castrating black woman is common in the movies and on television. She is physically imposing, usually shown standing with her hands on her hips, berating some cowering black man for his failings in the masculinity department. Her voice is shrill and would make anyone within ten feet of her shudder.

Such a woman is called a Sapphire after the character in the old *Amos and Andy* radio and television series. Sapphire was the wife of the Kingfish, a scheming, manipulating man who was constantly getting himself into trouble and testing Sapphire's patience. He wasted their money and never kept his promises. That Sapphire got fed up with his antics is not surprising. Yet to this day her name is synonymous with negative behavior in black women, as if she *should* have been demure and submissive while her husband put the family's well-being at risk.

Black women hate the term Sapphire so much that they fail to see that a Sapphire is really acting out because her man is not respecting, appreciating, or desiring her. A woman who is provoked into a Sapphire mode is usually panicked about her situation, stuck without resources, or fearful of abandonment. She may tolerate, tolerate, and tolerate some more, until finally the dam breaks—and anyone who gets in her way is going to hear what she has to say or else. But instead of articulating her fear or despair, she often explodes into a rage over something relatively insignificant. This causes her man to complain that she is attacking his manhood; a commonly heard term is "ball buster." The insult incenses Sapphire even more—and hardens her resolve to keep what is really bothering her locked deep inside.

Black women are not grenades that go off for pleasure (as many black men think). Most women try hard to avoid getting angry, especially at their loved ones. But they also feel that they get little attention until they scream and yell. They want to "nicely" ask for what they want, but they also want an immediate and positive response. So they wind up yelling. By nagging or complaining about surface concerns while unresolved issues simmer underneath, women stay locked in hopeless battles with their men.

Home, like the outside world, is a pressure cooker. Sapphire strives to keep up with her parenting responsibilities, aware that she will be criticized if things go wrong with the children—but that her man will not. If he walks out, Sapphire will be blamed for being too demanding. If he stays, he'll carp that she is unsupportive, even though she works day and night to physically, financially, and emotionally support her family. Sapphire screams not only for herself but for all black sisters who put up with too much.

Mothers to the World

Estelle made a stunning entrance into my office. She wore a full-length mink coat set off with designer bag and shoes. Her hair was perfectly coiffured and her makeup looked impeccable, as though it had just been done professionally. Yet she seemed oddly listless; no smile or vitality brightened her beautiful facade. She stared at me in silence for what seemed an extremely long time (most of my clients begin immediately to pour out their troubles). I asked what brought her into my office and she seemed uncertain as to how to proceed.

Estelle began by describing her lavish lifestyle. She had a beautiful suburban home that she had painstakingly decorated herself, a top-of-the-line Mercedes (a birthday present from her husband), and membership in exclusive clubs. She kept busy by shopping and going to balls and luncheons. I wondered what any of this had to do with why she came to see me.

With tremendous shame and embarrassment she divulged the miseries of her marriage to Randolph, one of Washington's most prominent officials. For several years he had been seeing—and supporting—another woman, Caroline, with whom he shared vacations and many, many weekends. Estelle had discovered recently that some of their friends not only knew about Caroline but that she had acted as hostess for some private dinners that Randolph held at the condominium he had bought for her. While he attended many social functions with his wife, Caroline often showed up with another escort at the same affairs.

When he was home, Randolph paid little attention to Estelle. Their encounters had become brief and superficial. He might ask about the children or some social obligation, but usually he closed himself off in his private den where he did paperwork, listened to music, watched television, or used the phone. He would come out to get a snack before going to bed and that was about it. Often Estelle was in the house and never really saw him. What she wanted from me was an explanation of her husband's behavior and a plan to get him to love her again and to leave Caroline.

I stopped Estelle about ten minutes before our session was to end and asked her why we had spent almost forty minutes talking about her husband and no time talking about her. I wanted to know what she wanted for herself, because all I had heard about was Randolph: his likes and dislikes, how he required an efficiently run home and well-behaved kids, how generous he was with his money, and how much fun he was when he wanted to be.

"Estelle, why do you choose to spend your time in therapy focusing entirely on someone else?" I asked. "Don't you think you should want to know something about your own behavior and why you choose to put up with such offensive treatment?" I told Estelle that only when she learned more about herself would she be able to define the choices she could make.

"I've always enjoyed taking care of people," Estelle mused. "I virtually raised my younger sister and I didn't mind doing it. I felt honored at college when my friends made late night stops at my dorm room to discuss their problems with me. It meant a lot to me to try to help, and I still do this for my friends. Randolph used to love the way I took care of him and the family, but now he doesn't seem to notice or care. And what really hurts is that I know that Caroline is not like me at all."

Estelle was a well-educated, upper-class woman who lacked self-confidence and sound reality-testing abilities. She had always assumed that if she *gave* all she would *get* all, that the only way she could be worthy of love was if she gave selflessly. She was so self-sacrificing that it was almost inevitable she would be taken advantage of.

Like many black women, Estelle believed that being a "good woman" meant taking care of others and requiring little in return. Estelle raised Randolph's children, kept up his home, and expertly fulfilled the role of political wife, but though she gave and gave, she accepted her husband's blatant infidelity and humiliating behavior. And like many men, Randolph figured he had kept up much of the "bargain." He provided Estelle with a luxurious home, a closetful of designer clothes, two healthy children, and plenty of status in the community. If he had special needs of his own, surely he was entitled to meet them—since he continued to support Estelle in the manner to which she had loved becoming accustomed. That Estelle's years of devoted support had enabled him to rise so high in his profession was something Randolph chose not to acknowledge.

Estelle's situation may seem extreme, but the fundamentals are not so uncommon. Many black women are lifelong enablers. It makes sense to them to take care of others as they wish someone would care for them.

This tradition is rooted in the black culture where women have always reared the children and run the households—their own and others—whether men were present or not. It's ancestral; it's in their blood. Too late do many women recognize that a preoccupation with mothering to the exclusion of their own needs is detrimental to their own lives.

One of the most popular topics on my radio show was "Dependent Relationships: How to Crush Love." I was flooded with calls from black women who couldn't understand why their men had left them even after "they had done everything for them." One caller said she had tried to "grow her a man." I asked what she meant by this. She said, "You know, you meet a man who is nice, attractive, and takes you places, but he needs to grow up, mature, and develop himself more as a person. I work on him in stages, get him to take more initiative for himself, change his career focus, go to school, get a degree, and I also teach him about safe sex and good loving. Trouble is, once he's all grown up, he leaves me. I'm really tired of growing them, even though they depend on me to do so."

Women who believe that a man's dependency will translate into love and a permanent relationship are making a mistake. "Mothering women" firmly believe dependent men will always need and love them. Need, yes; love, no. By definition, a male who is "mothered" will eventually need to detach, to become independent and venture away from mommy.

I once spent a weekend at the New England home of friends. On Saturday night, we all decided to go out for dinner. With only two bathrooms in the house and ten guests, we were all running around trying to get some time in a bathroom. One of the women kept calling to her husband, who was playing video games with the kids, because she wanted him to hurry up and get into the shower. "I have already showered," he said. "Well, then come over here and let me smell you," she replied. I couldn't believe she was treating him like a little boy, and that he was willing to be treated like one. I wasn't surprised to hear a few months later that they had separated.

I recall a young woman who came into my office virtually hysterical. Jannelle's boyfriend of four years, Mark, had recently left her for another woman who was pregnant with his child. What amazed Jannelle was that Mark used to tell her that he couldn't stand to be without her. This was the kind of love she had been looking for all her life. Jannelle's parents had separated when she was young. Jannelle, an only child, had been the constant center of attention before her parents' separation. While they both loved her, after the separation neither seemed to have much time for her as they went about building new lives for themselves. She hungered for a man to compensate for her parents' neglect. She felt *entitled* to compensation.

Because Mark was so dependent on her initially, Jannelle felt that he was truly "the one" and that he would stay with her always. As time went on, he felt suffocated by her all-encompassing love. When she asked for a marriage proposal, he pulled back and ultimately out of the relationship. Now she was devastated. "I feel like nothing without this man. What am I to do? I feel so empty inside without someone to care for."

Jannelle spent her nonworking hours driving by Mark's house. She thought that if she could just get a glimpse of his new girlfriend, she could figure out why he had left her.

Jannelle's sense of entitlement was evident immediately in our first session. She wanted me to just listen to her and provide no feedback for a while. Then she wanted to extend our sessions to two hours instead of the traditional fifty minutes because she said she needed more of my attention. Jannelle was transferring her entitlement to me, as though my attention could make up for the deficit of attention she suffered as a child. After several months of therapy, Jannelle began to understand that she was trying to achieve what was not possible—an "ideal parent" who would make up for the childhood attention that was irretrievably lost. It *was* possible to find an attentive, loving partner, but he could not be expected to magically make the hurts of her childhood go away.

Black women must be careful not to buy into what black men say they want. Brothers often describe their ideal woman as one who will take care of them, be uncritical, and always be there for them no matter what they do. However, they often find such a woman boring and unchallenging, and quickly lose interest. They may hold on to her for some time for the services she can provide—housework, social status, sexual favors, or even paying his bills. Ultimately, however, they leave—and she doesn't even realize that giving him everything and asking for nothing, far from keeping him close, were what drove him away.

Woman to the Rescue

When "mothering" black women aren't propping up dependent men, they may try to find men who are in the midst of some crisis and need a woman to rescue them. It goes like this: he just lost his job, he's going to be evicted, he has a problem with his ex-wife or his kids; his car just broke down and he needs $1,000. The circumstances may range from life-threatening to trivial. She often receives a midnight call to come and get him because he is stranded in the next town with no way to get home. Being the rescuer—the ultimate "mommy"—she jumps up, gets dressed, and heads out the door.

The rescuer is not stupid or masochistic; she truly believes that she will get something in return. But feeling worthy of receiving is unfamiliar terrain for her, so she denies any needs of her own and opts instead to do the "taking care of." Her payoff, she assumes, is that as the giver she will get to call the shots.

Women often ask me why they fall so easily into the thankless role of rescuer. It is usually a matter of social conditioning. Often when these women were young, they had to be pleasing, sweet, and responsible in order to gain a parent's attention and (conditional) love. They made the unconscious connection that their pleasing and accommodating behavior would also attract and hold a man. By rescuing a man, they believe, they will "earn" his loyalty and he will feel grateful and obligated to stay forever. Hence, she will never be alone.

This behavior is appealing bait to black men who are seeking unconditional, loving mothers. The problem is that rescuers do have conditions, but they don't express them. The most obvious condition is a simple one: "Recognize the 'good' in me and love me, and never leave me."

Rescuing, like mothering, is not designed to be a permanent role. Nature provides children with mothers who help them grow emotionally and physically until they can live on their own and make responsible choices so that they will not *need* rescuing. If a woman is a successful mother or rescuer, her man will leave her, eventually, to go off on his own. If she is not successful, then she is stuck with a man in perpetual infancy. Eventually she is bound to become angry and tired of his dependent role.

Stand by Your Man: The Protector

The protector is the black woman who protects her man in order to keep him by her side. She will deny there is any problem in their relationship, and if there is a problem, she will take care of it. A woman may do this because she cannot bring herself to acknowledge that her newfound love may not be what he seems. She might notice that he drinks too much, but she will look the other way. She will call his office to tell his boss that he is home sick when he is actually nursing a hangover. She will return a suit he bought and insist on getting his money back. By protecting him, she protects her investment. The dividend she expects is unending loyalty.

Many protectors are women with other problems of their own. Often they connect with partners around mutual suffering and mistake this joining for true love.

Marian was a thirty-year-old woman with one small child. She had a well-paying job as an assistant manager of a small clothing boutique and was learning so much about the merchandising business that she planned one day to own and operate her own store. Her latest love, Theo, was a cocaine addict who promised her repeatedly that he was going to break his habit. Theo spun long stories about why he couldn't make it in the white man's world and how desperately he needed her support. Here's the whammy: *he said that he needed her in order to be the man they both wanted him to be.* Because he needed her, Marian thought he loved her, even though their life together was totally unsatisfying—in fact, hellish.

Loving and hurting had always been tightly intertwined for Marian. She was raised in a family in which emotional and physical abuse were common, sometimes daily, occurrences. Her mother took care of—protected—Marian's alcoholic father, who always seemed to be between jobs. Marian grew up believing that sacrificing for and protecting men were normal things for a woman to do.

Ironically, Marian found Theo's neediness reassuring. Any man in such bad shape surely wouldn't walk out on her. She told all her friends that he was going to stop using cocaine, and she was determined to make him do so. What Marian did not understand was that neither she nor anyone else could make him give up drugs; he had to want to get clean, and he had to do it himself. Even if it were possible for her to help him kick the habit, he would not necessarily need or want her afterwards.

Marian told me she stayed with Theo because he had such potential. Perhaps he was, indeed, a diamond in the rough, a prince in addict's clothing. But no matter how great Theo's potential may have been, he could never meet Marian's deepest need: on a subconscious level, she wanted Theo to give her the love her father never did. No man, not even a genuine prince, can fill the love gaps of childhood. By seeking out a man like her father, Marian was dooming herself to repeat her mother's cheerless life.

In therapy Marian learned that truly loving Theo—and herself— meant letting go of her twin fantasies: that she could change him, and that he could make up for her childhood pain. She also realized that she had to stop protecting him so that he could face his addiction with good professional help.

Self-Reliance: A Blessing or a Curse?

Many black women are self-reliant because as children they were encouraged by loving parents to be independent, responsible, and judicious in their decision making. Yet for other women, self-reliance grew out of a rueful awareness that even as children, they had to learn quickly to take care of themselves.

In my doctoral research on self-efficacy among women, I interviewed hundreds of black female government workers in the Washington, D.C., area. Most reported that early childhood experiences pushed them into becoming self-reliant and independent. Some were even forced into being co-parents, responsible for caring for one or more of the other children in the family. Some had lost parents through death or divorce, and felt that they had to grow up faster than other children their age.

Pauline, a forty-eight-year-old woman who owns a computer firm, typifies their experiences. Pauline grew up on welfare in a family of nine children. Her survival as a kid had depended upon her decision-making abilities and her deeply felt sense of responsibility. There were few financial resources, and much of the time both parents were out of the home. It fell to Pauline to take care of herself and the other children. She remembers fixing meals of cold-cut sandwiches because she was too small to reach the stove. She ran errands, and eventually the neighborhood grocer got to know her and helped her with her shopping list. When Pauline was in junior high school, she had to go to her brother's elementary school to bail him out of trouble. She knew what to say to the school principal and quickly learned how to negotiate all kinds of issues that came up for her siblings. In high school and then in a special program for welfare-dependent high school graduates, Pauline acquired computer skills, eventually becoming so recognized for her expertise that she founded a successful business.

While these experiences taught Pauline to be self-reliant, they also overdeveloped her "masculine" side. Pauline did not get the opportunity to rely on others, to feel cared for enough that she could develop her "feminine" side. Pauline was now a self-assured and accomplished adult, but her personal life was in ruins. All her life, her parents had told her, "Trust no one to support you." Pauline drove herself to develop her business at the expense of her marriage. Her husband, a bus driver, felt so neglected and fed up with her long hours at the office, as well as the briefcase full of paperwork that she brought home, that he began to have an affair.

All her life Pauline had wanted a consistent partner and now that she had one, he was unfaithful. John wanted her to give him as much time as she gave to her job; his own mother was home when he was small, and he was not used to the "mother" in the household being away so much. His infidelity was his way of "acting out" against the mother who was not acting like one. John didn't realize that Pauline's workaholism was not rejection of him but the realization of all she had been groomed to be as a child.

For months, Pauline and I worked on developing more balance within herself, letting her softness and dependence come through, while managing the independent and aggressive traits. As she learned to trust the process and me, she developed new skills for addressing vulnerability. She learned to speak more openly about her fears, to ask for what she wanted more directly, and to allow others in her life to know when she was sad or in need of nurturance. In time, Pauline was able to share these new experiences with John, not by talking but by demonstrating new behaviors and attitudes. The first issue they tackled together was how hurt she was by his affair. Incredibly, in all their years of marriage, John had never seen Pauline cry or appear anything but in control.

Pauline's situation reminded me of a *Washington Post* essay, "Why Are Black Women Scaring Off Their Men?" in which Joy Jones effectively summed up the dilemma of self-reliant black women: "What I have found, and what many of these women have yet to discover, is that the skills that make one successful in the church, community or workplace are not the skills that make one successful in a relationship. . . . It requires making decisions that not only gratify you, but satisfy others. It means doing things that will keep the peace rather than achieve the goal, and sometimes it means creating the peace in the first place."

A growing number of black women are so hostile toward black men that they have sworn off them like a bad habit. They claim that "black men are worthless! Hopeless!" They go it alone or explore romantic liaisons with women. They see their married sisters as hapless victims of circumstance, and pity those single women who bemoan their "manless" state. The sour-grapes complex has claimed these sisters; because they haven't found a good man they assert that no good men are out there to find. They say they're just being realistic. I believe they're being defensive. They openly reject their desire for a man in order to avoid the painful, disappointing truth: they want what they think they can't have.

I am convinced that most black women long to be in a relationship with a black man. Just look at the tremendous amount of time and energy black women spend discussing this issue in therapy and with women friends. Obviously, romance with a man is deeply important to them. When women clients tell me they have given up on men, I urge them to explore whether in fact they have made peace with not having a man in their lives, or whether they are just offering a sophisticated defense in order to get by.

I know that black women get tired of the endless games that seem to accompany partnerships with black men. After ten or twenty years of dating, some decide that it is just easier to drop out of the male–female social scene and declare that "there aren't any good ones anyway."

At a workshop I led recently in Atlanta, one woman expressed her disgust with the dating scene: "Someone said to me that women play too many games. But black women have to play games. If we don't, the men will. What you have to do is go ahead and play for a little while so he will know that you understand the game. Then maybe he will respect you, and y'all can move on to better things. But if he thinks that he has an 'airhead' or 'pushover' who is going to do anything for him because he's so wonderful, he is gonna just run over you, get his little stuff taken care of, and move on about his business. And that, ladies, is a fact."

Some black women have heard all of their lives that sex is the only reason a woman needs a man; other than that, women do just fine by themselves. At one of my workshops in San Francisco, a young black woman told the group, "I hear my father's voice in my head all the time saying, 'No one is going to do anything for you, you've got to get out there, get the job, and do it for yourself.' " With this well-learned lesson playing repeatedly in her head, she had decided that no black man will do for her.

Katherine, forty-nine years old and twice divorced, fully agreed. "I've had it. Black men want too much. They are just a burden, and I am not going to weigh myself down. I remember the other night, while I was climbing the stairs to my bed after a long day at the office, all I could think was, thank God there is no one waiting for me upstairs." She laughed heartily, and the group laughed with her. But underneath the laughter, I heard wistfulness.

Is Relating White All Right?

Some black women have decided that the only answer to the shortage of good black men is a relationship with a white man. In a workshop I conducted on "How to Find Love," one black woman said she was tired of waiting for some black man to truly appreciate her.

"I don't care about the flack," she said. "The brothers have a nerve to give me evil looks when I'm out with my white friend, but I don't care. I waited for years for a black man and what did I get? Nothing but a lot of demands and trouble. I've had my femininity in storage, and now I've found a whole new experience."

Jackie, a forty-year-old administrator in a large urban hospital in the Midwest, has been married for four years to Milton, a Jewish man she met at a professional conference. This is Jackie's second marriage; the first was to a black man with whom she had two children.

"Milton is my friend, supporter, and lover. His color has nothing to do with us getting together. Most men—whether they're black, white, green, yellow, or purple—want the same things: power, control, and a woman to take care of them. If a man relates to me with respect and honesty, color is a nonissue."

When I asked if there weren't some differences between black men and white men, she responded that "white men are probably freer to express their feelings without a lot of macho posturing. Milton can be warm and sensitive with me without feeling that he is less of a man. But then he does have an advantage over a black man in that no one in this society would ever question his manhood since he has white skin. I know the brothers struggle with this issue, but I just cannot allow them to work out their masculinity problems on me. I don't have the patience for the games that go along with the black man's search for his manhood."

Some of Jackie's black female friends were critical when she chose to marry Milton. They asked how she could sleep with a white man knowing what white men have done to black women over the years. "People have to understand that I feel entitled to have a loving mate and that's it," Jackie said firmly. "The fact that he is white should not matter. I did not marry a white man; I married a man who loves me."

Paul, a white man I interviewed, said unequivocally that black women are the sexiest, most exotic women on the face of the earth. "I am not likely to be turned on by a blue-eyed blond," he said. "Black women make me feel desirable and stroke me emotionally." He married a black woman and didn't care that some people disapproved. Admitting that they receive stares from both blacks and whites when they are out, he said, "She is so beautiful to me. I can't worry about what people think."

More than once I have heard black women say that white men more openly affirmed their feminine beauty. I believe this affirmation is especially significant for black women who have often felt rejected by their own men because their skin was not the "right" color, or their hair was not long enough, or their bodies were more full than thin. Writer Audrey Edwards addressed this issue in an essay, "Sleeping with the Enemy."

The first man to ever tell me I was beautiful was white. A photographer. In Tacoma, Washington. I don't remember exactly why he happened to be at my mother's house, but I do remember him saying when we were introduced, "My God, you should be in *Vogue.*" I was seventeen then, bone thin, wearing a batiked mini-dashiki. "Stunning" is the word I believe he used.

Five years later, at a party in Seattle, I was standing around with the other black women that evening feeling very un-stunning. We were watching the brothers present dancing with the white women present. It was a routine occurrence in a town that would later earn the distinction of having the highest incidence of inter-racial unions of any city in the country. That summer night, however, before time and distance gave me some perspective and success gave me confidence, I took the behavior of the brothers personally, and gave in to the brooding self-hatred typical of so many black women who grow up under the proverbial ugly stick. I was too dark, too tall, too full-featured, too short-haired—too un-white—to be beautiful, to be desired.

Although more and more black women are dating and marrying white men, there are still many who believe that this choice makes them traitors to the race. Tamara, a forty-four-year-old teacher, spoke rather nostalgically about a wonderful relationship she had years ago with a white man.

"I loved him and I know that he loved me," she said. "But ultimately I couldn't make the commitment to him. I felt too guilty every time we were together, and I was embarrassed to take him home to my folks or to introduce him to my friends. We couldn't make a life together with me feeling all of this conflict, so we had to part. I still miss him a great deal, and we get together from time to time, but it will never be the same. He didn't understand why I couldn't go the distance with him. I still wonder if I made the right decision, since I still don't have anything solid with a black man."

Black men are far less reluctant to explore relationships with white women than black women are with white men, or with men of other races and cultures. I sense, however, that this situation will change. Until the man shortage begins to abate, I predict that more black women will look to men of various ethnic groups for love, marriage, and family options. While most black women seem to truly prefer black men, they may be unwilling to let the man shortage narrow their choices.

Staying Hopeful

With all the difficulties that black women face, I am always heartened to meet those who have accepted that while they would dearly love to share their life with a man, they are moving ahead to build productive, fulfilling lives for themselves. "Staying hopeful" is how Lisa, a pharmaceutical sales manager, described her attitude.

"I have been lucky to have some really good relationships with black guys even though they didn't last all that long," she told me. "I don't like to generalize about men because they are all different. Even though my love life is still in limbo, I still believe that eventually I will meet the right man."

Lisa, thirty-nine years old, had never married. She worked long hours and attended graduate school part time to earn her M.B.A. Her biggest thrill was her three-year-old adopted daughter, who was born to a distant cousin who couldn't raise her. Lisa had always wanted children, and just when she had despaired of having a child of her own, her mother mentioned this little girl who desperately needed a stable home environment. Lisa immediately set about rearranging her life. She was now consumed with finding the right preschool, taking the youngster to the park on weekends, and sharing motherly stories with other women in the neighborhood.

"Having this child with me has changed my life," Lisa said with a huge smile on her face. "My hair and nails don't get done too often, and I'm not in the stores like I used to be. I am saving every dime to buy a house with a big yard for my baby and me. I have never been more exhausted in my whole life, but she and I are just having the best time, and the future couldn't look better."

Lisa's decisions were not made in retaliation or bitterness; she genuinely liked men and hoped for a relationship to develop. But she took full responsibility for building a life she could feel good about; she was fully aware that if anyone was entitled to make her happy, it was herself.

Life cannot be put on hold. With or without a man, a woman has to move on.

6

Love Games, Power Plays, and Sexual Defenses

Her Side	His Side
[Men] turned out to be a major disappointment. Said one thing and did another. Couldn't back up half of what they'd led me to believe. Then begged me to be patient. And like a fool, I tried it, until I got tired of idling, and the needle fell on empty. They wanted to play house. Or The Dating Game. Or Guess Where I'm Coming From? or Show Me How Much You Love Me Then I'll Show You. And then there're the ones who got scared when they realized I wasn't playing. "You're too intense," one said. "Too serious," said another.	[Women] are all the same, that's for damn sure. Want all your time and energy. Want the world to revolve around them. Once you give 'em some good lovin', they go crazy. Start hearing wedding bells. . . . Every time I turned around, my phone was ringing off the damn hook. "Hi, Franklin," one would say. And I would sit there and try to guess which one it was. "Whatcha doing?" What a stupid-ass question to call somebody up and ask. It oughta be obvious that I wasn't thinking about her, or else I'da called her, right?

—TERRY MCMILLAN,
Disappearing Acts

The battle for love and power is fueled by a belief that both men and women share: *the opposite sex has more power.* In order to survive, the thinking goes, one has to be psychologically armed; otherwise, there's the risk of being conquered and overtaken. Although "in love" is the opposite of "on guard," many people cling to the defenses that they feel will protect them. Through love games they toy with people's hearts, pretending that love is just a transient thing that doesn't matter that much anyway. Through power plays people struggle to hold on to their sense of control; they claim to be committed to a relationship, but at the same time they defend against getting too close. These maneuvers only distance them from the love they say they want. They also perpetuate the illusion that a person can love without being vulnerable. Love means *embracing* vulnerability while at the same time remaining intact and whole.

The idea of allowing themselves to be vulnerable is very threatening to many black men and women. They often say they don't feel "safe" in love. What will happen if I trust too much? Will I be mocked? Betrayed? What if I get close and then can't get out of it? What if I lose myself to love—can I ever get myself back? What if my partner is leading me on, and then I get dependent, and then my partner leaves?

Owing to the gender-role confusion described in chapter 2, men often fear that needing love (allowing their "soft side" to show) will diminish their masculinity, and women fear that expressing their desire to be protected will leave them too "at risk" and disappointed. The goal for both sexes is to blend their masculine and feminine sides, to allow themselves to be soft *and* safe *and* strong. A healthy, interdependent relationship opens up to both partners the entire spectrum of human potential, the full range of feelings.

Sometimes men and women's feelings of entitlement give them unrealistic expectations of love. If they expect a partner to be the rescuer, the hero, the mama or daddy they've always wanted, they are setting themselves up for major disappointment. No one can compensate for the hurts of the past. If they expect a relationship to give them a power base—a chance to balance the scales after a life of being ordered around, bullied, overlooked, or abused—they are setting themselves up for loneliness.

Throughout the search for love, sex, of course, is a constant presence. Ideally, sex involves genuine desire and passion, a way to express love. But sometimes sex is used as a tool—to lead someone on, to connect physically but stay detached emotionally, to withhold love while seeming to offer it. Or sex may be used as a mask—a way to attract a lover and hide at the same time.

And sometimes sex is a consolation prize for people who despair of ever finding true intimacy. If they can't have the "real thing," then at least they won't have to settle for nothing at all. Rather than being an expression of desire, love, or connection, sex for them is an expression of fear and hopelessness.

Self-Sabotage Through Fantasy

It's fine to dream, to fantasize about what an ideal mate might be like. But it is crucial to know the difference between wishful thinking and realistic assessment. People often imagine that attraction is love, that affection is commitment, that potential is actual. In their blind, headlong urgency to find a partner, they often make self-sabotaging judgments that ultimately produce the opposite of what they really want and need.

The Quantum Leap

Dorothea, a thirty-year-old medical researcher, came to me in tears after her fiancé broke off their engagement. After years of disappointing relationships with men, she had thought she'd finally found "the one" who would make her dreams of a fantasy wedding and "happily ever afters" finally come true. These dreams had fallen through before, and now she was humiliated that they had shattered yet again.

"All my life I've wanted to get married," she told me. "Even through graduate school and all of these years on the job, I have always known that getting married and having a family were my main goals. I could give up this job tomorrow if only I could find the right man."

Dorothea was so obsessed with finding a husband that in the months to come, I could tell the status of her love life by observing how she walked into my office. If she had just met a promising man, she had an extra bounce in her step; when the relationship fell through, as they all did sooner or later, Dorothea dragged herself through my door and sagged into a chair. She allowed her man search to dominate her life and preclude all other possibilities of enjoyment.

Dorothea's mother, aunt, and grandmother raised her to believe that no matter how much a woman achieved, she wasn't worth much without a man.

"When Mom had a man in the picture, she would sing and dance around and the whole household would be full of life," Dorothea recalled. "But when her relationships didn't work out, she was so gloomy she couldn't even stand to cook a meal. My brothers and I always ate better when Mom had a boyfriend."

Dorothea was obviously replicating her mother's behavior. And because she denied herself any feeling of well-being unless she had a man, she leaped into making a commitment before a man was ready to make one to her.

One day Dorothea practically skipped into my office, and I knew she'd met somebody. Percy, she announced, was the new man of her dreams. He was handsome, with large, melting eyes, and had a great job as a research and development manager for a large corporation. Every week she divulged more about Percy: he made delicious lasagna, he took her to three movies in a row, he invited her to his office picnic.

Two months after meeting Percy, Dorothea almost floated into my office. Her radiant smile lit up the room.

"You will never guess what happened! Percy got this great job offer in Dallas, and he told me he's going to take it. The company is going to provide him a place to stay, a car, and great trips abroad. I can't believe how great this is."

As Dorothea raved about Percy's job offer, I waited patiently to see what his job offer had to do with her obvious euphoria. I found it difficult to understand why his leaving town would make her so happy.

"Are you planning to go with him?" I asked.

"Yes," she said. "I am moving to Texas!"

I was shocked by her plan because they had known each other such a short time. Although they saw each other often, nothing she had told me suggested that they were ready to move in together.

After some prodding, Dorothea admitted that Percy had not actually asked her to accompany him to Dallas.

"He said we would still see each other, and made me promise I would still be his girl," Dorothea said. "You should have seen the sad look on his face, Audrey. I know he can't stand the thought of leaving me. So after thinking about him all weekend, I decided to surprise him and tell him that I will go with him. After all, he's the man I love and it's up to me to prove it."

We talked about her decision at length. I urged her to reconsider moving to another city with a man who had made no commitment to her. Yet Dorothea had no qualms; she was certain that Percy loved her.

Several weeks later, Dorothea called to cancel her appointment. Her voice on the phone was flat and lifeless, and she made vague excuses about why she couldn't come in. The next week, and the week after that, she canceled her sessions again.

When at last Dorothea shuffled in, she looked like a woman who had lost everything. She was so despondent, she even talked about wanting to end her life.

"You will never believe what Percy said to me," Dorothea sobbed. "I thought he would be thrilled when I told him I would move to Dallas with him. Instead he got an attitude. He said it was a stupid idea to quit my job and move just because he was. He said he had plenty of frequent flyer credits and would commute. I was crying so hard, finally he told me to just grow up and get a life."

I acknowledged Dorothea's pain, but pointed out that she had placed herself in a vulnerable situation. Although she and Percy had had a good time together, not once had he done or said anything to indicate that he wanted to live with her. Yet she almost willfully misinterpreted him, as if she listened through a filter of wishful thinking. If Percy said, "I miss you," she took this to mean that he loved her. If he said, "I need to be with you," she took this to mean that he couldn't live without her. She fantasized the relationship into what she wanted it to be.

Dorothea's distorted view led her to take a "quantum leap"—a grossly unwarranted jump to the conclusion that her desperate search for a partner was finally over. By letting her fantasies cloud reality, Dorothea was not only willing to change her life around for a man whom she knew casually; she also turned him off and thwarted any chance that, in time, their relationship could develop at normal speed.

After months of therapy, Dorothea was able to see how her desperate attempts to avoid her mother's loneliness had led her to reenact her mother's history. Over time, Dorothea found healthier ways to confirm and express her identity. She worked hard for a job promotion, improved her financial status, bought a house, and joined a prestigious medical team at a national health institute. No longer did she feel that she had to merge with a man in order to feel like an accomplished and worthy individual. She became able to relate to men in more realistic ways—not to reinforce who she was but rather to enhance the life she had made for herself.

Sex Will Make Everything All Right

Glenda, a forty-seven-year-old secretary at a consulting firm, became a client of mine after a sexual relationship with a man with whom she was virtually obsessed came to a sudden end. Glenda and Rick, one of the firm's new hires, were only cordial "water cooler" acquaintances until she was assigned to work with him on a special project. Glenda found Rick attractive, and had heard around the office that Rick was "quite something in the sack." She was disappointed that although he was charming and easy to work with, he never came on to her. That all changed one night when they were working late. To Glenda's delight, Rick finally made his move, and they made passionate love on the desk in his office. "I have to admit," Glenda later told me, "that he was indeed a stud."

After that night he asked her out a few times, then began coming by her apartment late at night. She didn't care how late he arrived or that he was always gone by morning and never wanted her for anything except sex.

When I pressed Glenda about her expectations for this relationship, she maintained that she was in love and would do anything to win this man—including answering her doorbell at midnight and letting him into her bed. But after weeks of late-night rendezvous, she was distraught when Rick told her that he loved having lots of women and didn't think he could ever settle down with just one.

Glenda had truly believed that if she made herself available to Rick whenever he wanted her, eventually he would decide that he couldn't do without her. I told her that she had obviously forgotten a most important dictum: the more you chase a distancer, the more distant they will become. Rick was a classic distancer—someone invested in not getting close to anyone. Distancers often sexualize their connections with women as a way to avoid becoming emotionally involved.

Things for Glenda went from bad to worse. Rick soon started cutting back on his time with her, and Glenda made reckless attempts to "get him back." She left countless, rambling messages on his answering machine, hoping to disturb anything Rick might be doing with another woman. Like the Glenn Close character in the film *Fatal Attraction*, Glenda stayed up around the clock, dialing Rick's number endlessly. Rick finally confronted her and said he wanted nothing more to do with her, not even sex. This was a real blow. Despite Rick's increasing distance, Glenda had persisted in believing that the sex between them was so intensely powerful that he would never give it up no matter what she did.

Glenda and I worked very hard to help her unravel the mystery of why she thought this relationship could ever become permanent. Glenda came to realize that she used sex to overcome her low self-esteem and shaky sense of femininity. Her oldest sister, Sally, who had raised her, had been depressed over some man for as long as Glenda could remember, leading Glenda to conclude that true love is an intrinsically troubled and depressing experience. Like Sally, Glenda mistook "hot sex" for true love, deluding herself into thinking that a man who made love to her would eventually pledge love beyond the bedroom. She believed that once a man finally gave her the love she felt entitled to, she could at last feel better about herself.

In therapy Glenda began to look at who she was, what she thought of herself as a woman. She learned to stop tearing away at what she thought of as her shortcomings: her looks, complexion, hair, figure. She thought about Sally in a new way; Sally's style of relating to men did not have to be Glenda's; low self-esteem was a passed-down trait, but not a genetic one, and Glenda could learn to feel better about herself.

Glenda changed her approach to love. When she met a man, she took time to get to know him, and set limits by not rushing the sexual element of the relationship. She took responsibility for her own behavior—and protected the self she was beginning to like.

When an individual consents to being used as a sexual object, the likelihood is that a partner will do exactly that, thereby eliminating the very thing the individual wants—a love relationship. Often men and women complain about being trapped in a role, but they don't recognize that they have really set up a situation that they also have the power to change. "You get back what you put out," the saying goes.

Pursuing the Uncatchable Catch

Some people enjoy being pursued; others enjoy being the pursuer. Problems arise when an individual constantly gets locked into one of these roles to his or her detriment.

Barbara, a forty-six-year-old management consultant, came to me for counseling because after enduring a seemingly endless cycle of unfulfilling relationships, she now seemed to be pursuing yet another. Bryce, the man she thought she was in love with, was a high-powered executive with a large corporation. He traveled a great deal and had many women whom he saw at his convenience. Since Barbara had always dreamed of being on the arm of a rich and powerful man, she was willing to play this hopeless game—even though in the back of her mind she knew she could never come out a winner.

While Barbara chased Bryce, Jake, a co-worker, pursued Barbara. Jake had asked her out many times, but she always turned him down because she wasn't sure if she found him attractive. Yet she complained to me constantly about sitting home on weekends with nothing to do. Eventually, I persuaded her to give Jake a chance—and before long she was smiling at how often she had turned down this man who was to become her mate.

"Jake is such a crucial part of my life now," she says. "I can't believe how I acted. Bryce treated me awful, but he was so glamorous I kept hoping it would work out. The guessing games with Bryce were agonizing, but they made him seem intense and exciting. I never knew when he would show up. Sometimes he would come for the weekend, and it would be heaven. Other times he would promise to visit, and never arrive. No call. No nothing. Once we were supposed to meet out of town and I waited for him at the train station for hours. He never showed up and I finally got back on the train and cried the whole way home. Now I can always depend on coming home to Jake. Maybe he's not as exciting as Bryce, but that kind of excitement I don't need anymore. I just need Jake."

Barbara realized that a rich but neglectful partner ultimately left her feeling emotionally impoverished—and that a healthy, wholesome, loving relationship was more valuable than all the riches in the world.

Holding Pattern

Jackson was deeply troubled by his inability to achieve an erection with his wife, Jayla, from whom he had been separated several months. They had continued to have sexual relations after they separated because they still hoped to work things out and get back together.

"I've always seen myself as a stud, and until I married Jayla, I always had lots of women," said Jackson, a slightly built man in his late forties. "I used to be able to handle ten women a month. Now here I am not even able to get it up with my own wife. I don't know what's wrong with me."

I had to prod Jackson to tell me about his relationship with Jayla. She had married Jackson because she thought his catering business would be so profitable that she would not have to work; she had always wanted to be a "lady of leisure." Within the last year or so, however, the recession had killed off much of his business. Groups he usually relied on for contracts had scaled back their social affairs, and developing new contacts was a slow and arduous process. Yet Jackson felt sure that if he could just hold on, the business would turn around and become profitable again.

But Jayla was tired of hearing, "Wait, wait, wait for things to get better." She wanted him to get another job and do the catering on the side, but Jackson refused to consider it. They had endless fights about what she couldn't afford now that he was making less money, and about how "stupid" he was to keep trying to breathe new life into a dying business. Jayla felt entitled to a comfortable lifestyle, and berated Jackson for her feelings of deprivation. Yet she was willing to use him sexually because she had no other outlets for her sexual desires.

Jayla's mixed signals made Jackson feel continually less confident and less manly.

"I just can't relax around her anymore," Jackson said. "I am tired of fighting. The final straw was when she started telling me to hurry up in bed and get my needs over with so she could go to sleep. I did this a few times because I really wanted her, but eventually I just stopped asking."

When I asked Jackson why he continued to have sex with his wife, he replied, "I guess I keep hoping that if I can please her a little in bed we can keep this thing together long enough for me to prove I can make the money she wants."

Jayla clearly had Jackson "by the balls," as he put it; in fact, he once "slipped" and referred to her as a "ball breaker." She kept him in a holding pattern so he could satisfy her sexual needs, but put him down for being unable to satisfy her financial needs. Although Jackson was willing to let Jayla use him, Jackson's *body* was clearly rebelling. Yet not until Jackson discussed the situation in therapy did he make the direct connection between the conflict with Jayla and his failure to maintain an erection with her. He had assumed that he would never be able to perform sexually with *any* woman. Once he gave up the fantasy that Jayla would eventually come to accept and love him, Jackson was able to end their relationship—and regain his own sense of self, as well as his sexual abilities.

Dangerous Liaisons

Some people feel that truly exhilarating romance must include an element of risk or drama; in fact, they feel entitled to that kind of intensity, and some mistake intensity for love. They fantasize that living on the edge is the most romantic and desirable love; danger defines their passion.

Flora was the only daughter of the president of a chain of successful medical centers. His wife was a society matron who had scant interest in home and family life, so he took it upon himself to keep his daughter happy. He bought her a roomful of toys, sent her to expensive schools and summer camps, and ordered a local department store to keep her wardrobe chic and up-to-date. In return, he asked only that she please him with good grades and exemplary behavior. While her father was an extravagant provider, he traveled frequently and spent little time with her. So Flora grew up materially well off but emotionally neglected. Now in her mid-thirties, she had spent all of her adult life dating well-to-do men of questionable backgrounds but with large bank accounts; to Flora, wearing designer clothes, taking vacations abroad, and living in a luxurious condo made up for what she was missing emotionally.

Chuck came into her life one evening at a club known locally as a high-rollers' hangout. He was a fabulous dresser and a smooth conversationalist, and had a definite flair with women. Flora was delighted when he invited her to join him and some friends on his yacht one Sunday.

When Flora arrived at the dock, Chuck greeted her warmly and escorted her on to an empty deck. They were soon joined by a waiter whose sole purpose was to serve the two of them for the evening. Flora was dazzled. The fact that she had been told by several friends that he was involved in illegal activities did not faze her. She loved his style and was flattered that he chose her.

They began to see each other regularly. From time to time Chuck mentioned that his ex-wife was giving him a hard time, and joked that he wanted to steal the kids from his wife and hide them away. Flora sympathized with Chuck's frustration and often echoed his complaints about "that awful woman."

One morning when Flora arrived at work, a co-worker came into her office and closed the door.

"How are you holding up?" the friend asked. Bewildered by the question, Flora said, "What are you talking about?"

"You obviously haven't seen the newspapers," her friend continued. "Chuck's ex-wife is dead and no one knows where the kids are. Someone shot her last night at her home, and he's telling the police he knows nothing about it." Flora immediately leapt to his defense and frantically called around to find him. Once he assured her that he was innocent, she was satisfied and vowed to stick by him "no matter what."

Chuck was never tried for the murder because of a lack of evidence, but everyone, including the police, believed that he was involved. Everyone, of course, did not include Flora, who held his every word as truth, even though he had hinted many times that he wanted his wife out of his life. Flora's family was sick about her involvement with this man, but she would listen to no one. She was intoxicated with his lifestyle, even though she knew he was dangerous. Romance with Chuck was a heady experience, and she was determined to keep it going.

As Flora continued in therapy, she began to gain insight into the connection between her unresolved feelings about her father and her obsessions with Chuck and money. The realization was painful, but slowly helped her move toward separating from Chuck. By letting go of her fantasy of what could be, she was at last able to face what was.

Games of Control

Controlling another person is the agenda of choice for men and women who are trying to work out unexpressed disappointments and frustrations. If they felt powerless during childhood, they'll even the score by grabbing power now. If they inwardly quake at anyone's discovering how truly vulnerable they feel, they'll protect themselves by holding the reins and never allowing anyone else a turn. For controllers, relationships are not opportunities for love but arenas of competition. Power plays run the gamut from subtle manipulations and head trips to revenge, harassment, or abuse.

Love as Ownership

When controllers decide that a partner is their "one and only" (whether the partner agrees to this status or not), they think they have the right to treat the partner like a personal possession. A controller's love is like a prison; every time the partner makes a move, the controller is like a warden who has to know where he or she is at all times.

When Denise first met Ryan, a college basketball coach, he seemed like a dream come true. He was tall, supple, and sexy, wined and dined her at all the best places, and best of all, showed genuine interest in her work as an assistant editor at a fashion magazine; indeed, everything Denise said or did fascinated him. How long had it been, Denise thought happily, since a man really wanted to know what she had done all day and ' where she was going tomorrow. It seemed a natural progression from going out, to going to bed, to having him move some of his clothes to her place, to talking on the phone several times a day and seeing each other every night.

But before too long, the "natural progression" took an unnatural turn. If Ryan called and Denise was out of the office, he left a message for her to page him the moment she returned. Denise and a few girlfriends had a longstanding practice of meeting for drinks every Friday after work, but Ryan insisted that she get together with him instead. Why should he have to wait to get his weekend started? Why did Denise insist on seeing women friends? Was she using them as an alibi—was she really straying with someone else? Ryan was setting limits and Denise was learning that she'd better adhere to them, or he would fly into a jealous rage. When Denise balked at accounting for all her time, Ryan accused her of being unfaithful or uncaring. When she toed the line, however, Ryan rewarded her by acting like the charming man she was attracted to in the first place.

After nearly a year of Ryan control, Denise felt like a marionette who was tired of being jerked around. She felt lonely, since he didn't like her to see or talk with friends, and she felt constantly on edge, afraid to offend him. Denise had waited a long time for love, and hated the prospect of ending her relationship with Ryan. Any time she brought up the subject of easing things off, he insisted, like the old Lou Rawls song, "You'll never find another love like mine."

In therapy Denise sought to understand why she was so willing to settle for an oppressive relationship. Why did she feel such desperation? She realized that being *possessed* by someone is antithetical to being *loved*, and that if, indeed, she fulfilled the prophecy of the Lou Rawls song, it was better to be alone than to feel suffocated. Denise did at last break up with Ryan. And she eventually found a better love than his.

Taming Your Woman

I know many black men who revel in stories about strong, independent black women that they have been able to bring "in line." The stronger the women's facade, the more satisfying a conquest it becomes for him. The old adage "the harder they come, the harder they fall" is the password of this game of pretend.

Juan, an African Nicaraguan, had been married for fifteen years to a strong African-American woman, Linda. He found her fascinating, but hated how opinionated, strong-willed, and demanding she could be. Early in the marriage he complained about her demands to a male friend, and the friend's response set him on a course of control: "Man, you got to figure out some techniques for 'handling' your woman. You got to tame that Sapphire."

"The American black woman is a unique breed—so aggressive and demanding," he said to me. What Juan didn't say was that Linda's strong sense of independence was a powerful challenge to his notion of manhood. He wanted to dominate her in order to make himself feel more powerful, even though he wasn't willing to face her head-on.

Juan decided that Linda was never going to cater to him and treat him like a king. So he sent back home to Nicaragua for Rosie, a maid who could provide him with the domestic services he could not live without. Now when his feet hit the floor in the morning, Rosie was there with his slippers. She laid out his clothes, prepared special breakfasts for him, and had his briefcase waiting at the door while Linda was still in bed.

Having a maid should have given Linda a break from Juan's complaining, but the opposite was true. He constantly reminded Linda of her inadequacies, lamenting that her inability to be a decent wife had forced him to spend the money to hire a maid. Juan twisted the situation around, making it seem that it was Linda's failings, rather than his own demands, that deprived them of the ability to afford some of the things Linda wanted, such as a bigger house and a new car.

Every time Linda asked for something—a new dress, a vacation— Juan said, "Okay, baby," then "forgot" to follow through. This was his way of retaliating for how she had disappointed him. When they were first married, Juan believed that if he met her demands, she would respond by doing some of the things he wanted, such as rising early in the morning to make him breakfast and see him off. Since she never did, and therefore "forced" him to hire the maid, he made sure that his empty promises kept her as frustrated as he was. Together, they lived in a limbo of unkept promises.

Because black men are afraid they won't get what they want by being direct with their women, they devise indirect methods of controlling them, and hope the women won't realize that they're being controlled. Juan kept his wife in a state of constant frustration, but some men control their women in a different way. They give their girlfriends or wives any material item they ask for but refuse to give anything of themselves emotionally.

Sex as Revenge Against Past Abuse

At a meeting of a black women's support group, one woman was astounded at the sexual exploits of another member, Mona.

"So you are having lots of sex, huh?" she questioned Mona.

"Yeah," Mona responded, "whenever I can get it."

The first woman shot back, "Girl, I haven't had sex in so long, I can't even remember what it's like."

In private sessions, Mona spoke with me about what sex meant to her.

"I have had lots of men," she said. "The older I get, the more comfortable I am with my own body and what gives me pleasure. I believe in total freedom in the bedroom and demand that my men act the same way. If they cannot satisfy me, they won't be seeing much of me. I need a man to make me feel wonderful, womanly, accepted, and satisfied. I am in total control of my sexuality."

Mona, who was in her mid-forties, taught English at a small college.

She was reluctant to talk much about her family background, but eventually disclosed that she had not grown up with her natural mother, who died of cancer. Her father worked very hard to provide for his child but he never felt comfortable rearing her alone, so he moved her around among different family members. Mostly, Mona remembered staying with Aunt Addie.

For a time Aunt Addie's house was a warm and welcoming retreat. Mona had fond memories of her aunt cuddling her and rocking her to sleep when she was feeling lonely for her mother. Yet one of her most traumatic experiences happened while she was under Aunt Addie's care. Uncle Wheeler was Addie's boyfriend and he was around the house a lot. He was very attentive to Mona, and she liked this since she didn't get to see her dad very much.

One night Mona was abruptly awakened by a large figure crawling into bed with her. When she heard the voice, it was familiar. It was Uncle Wheeler. He told her not to worry; he cared about her and would take care of her. Then he reached into her pajamas and started to fondle her in a way she had never felt before. He repeated the routine many nights after, but for years Mona had refused to acknowledge that this sexual abuse had ever happened. Only after months of therapy did Mona recall the experience and reflect on how it had affected her relations with men. Because Uncle Wheeler had destroyed her trust in men, she had not permitted herself to get close to any man. She would have sex only when it was on her terms, and she thrived on the tremendous rush of power that her control over a man gave her. Her life was dedicated to making sure that a man would never again hurt or control her.

"I like to get a man where I want him so I can have him anywhere and anytime that I want him," Mona liked to say. "It gives me pleasure to keep men dangling, waiting for me to decide whether and when sex will happen." Mona had her "revenge" on Uncle Wheeler, but ultimately it didn't make her feel any better. By replaying, again and again, a revised script of her past, Mona kept herself from feeling the true sexual gratification that comes only when sex is freely given, freely obtained.

I'm Not the Person I Make You Think I Am

I have often heard older women offer this advice to young women who are looking for a partner: "Be careful what you do in the beginning of a relationship because he will expect it forever. If you start out doing everything for him and pretend to expect nothing in return, nine times out of ten he will hold you to this agreement. Think about it before you start playing this game. It can backfire in a big way!"

But many people feel insecure that their true self is something anyone will want. A woman may fear disclosing her wish for an equal relationship—so she may "wait on a man" at first, and only later ask for some coddling herself. Or she may think a man would prefer an independent woman who doesn't need much, so she may act the part, then feel deprived when he is inattentive to her needs.

One of the most common personas both men and women assume is that of a sexual tiger or tigress—hot, ready, and very, very experienced. It's great to be sexual, and fine to be experienced—but many black men and women, often in response to stereotypes perpetuated by society, feel the need to "package" themselves like commodities on the market. It is always best to be oneself, to have the confidence to say, "What you see is what you get"—a wonderfully complex individual, full of human warmth as well as heat.

Bait and Switch

A male client once said to me, "I keep meeting women who claim to be so independent, but they are always in my back pocket. They say things like: 'I need some money. I don't want to take care of myself. I've been working since I was twelve years old and it ain't no fun. I don't get no thrills taking care of myself.' But when I first met these same women, they seemed proud of their work and independence. It gets so I don't know whether I can trust who a woman says she is."

"Bait and switch" is a con game merchandisers play. They'll advertise a certain appealing product, then when you show up in the store, they "just happen" to be out of it and try to sell you a different product instead, usually one that is inferior, more expensive, or not a name brand. Some people use a "bait and switch" routine to get a partner. They present a false image of themselves, then later reveal the actual "product."

"If I don't pretend to need nothing, black men will stay miles away from me," one woman told me. "Black men don't want high-upkeep women who demand lots of phone calls and dinners and roses. They want ladies who will cook them nice meals and give them great sex and who are pretty happy most of the time. Black men don't want to hear ladies' troubles. They have enough of their own."

A woman who pretends to be completely self-sufficient is setting herself up for disappointment. Men, understandably enough, will have taken the relationship on the terms she first presented, then balk openly when she tries to turn the tacit agreement on its head. They may, in fact, be baffled when she takes off her mask and starts asking for emotional support. Time and again, men have complained to me about women who "change up on them." No one likes to be tricked.

Agnes, an attractive woman in her late forties, came to me in distress because Kendall, a man she thought she loved, had skipped out on her. When she first met this sensual, attractive man, she flipped and decided to pull out all the stops. He was job hunting, he told her, and needed to look decent, so she charged a $400 suit for him with the understanding that he would pay her back. He needed a car to go to interviews, so she loaned him her BMW. She had no idea that he was driving her car all over town and had been issued numerous parking tickets.

One day, when leaving a shopping center, Agnes noticed a bright yellow boot on her car wheel. The police informed her that over $700 was owed in parking tickets, and until this amount was paid she couldn't move her car. She called her boyfriend's home in a panic to confront him, but no one answered his phone. In fact, the number had been disconnected. A mutual friend told her later that Kendall had left for California to work on a special project. At that point, she knew that she had been had.

Agnes had led Kendall to believe that she absolutely loved taking care of him and was loose about the money, but what she really wanted was a man who loved her and gave her as much as she gave him. She had privately fretted about running up her credit card bill, but hadn't wanted to chase him away by asking for repayment and seeming uptight. Eventually, of course, her own dishonesty with him compounded her pain: he had betrayed her, but she had *allowed* herself to be used. If she had spoken up earlier, he probably would still have skipped out, but at least she would have her pride—and her wallet—intact.

"Bait and switch" can also be a sexual game. When young black women sashay into my office radiating a seductive air, I often wonder how long they have cultivated this false image. I know they are attempting to overcompensate for their confused sense of femininity. Invariably these are the same women who complain to me that black men want them for only one thing. Although they resent feeling used sexually, they turn around and use their sexuality to attract men.

The game goes like this: a woman offers sex while keeping to herself her real desire to be loved and desired. Then she becomes angry when she gets exactly what she asked for—sex without any emotional ties. She resents men for how empty, guilty, and used she feels when the relationship does not give her the love she was craving all along.

Acting Out Sexual Stereotypes

Most African-American men and women are plagued by stereotypes and myths about black sexuality. For too long, black men have been seen as sex machines, studs, well-hung "Mandingos" who can thrill any woman with their strong virile moves. Black women have been depicted as Jezebels in short tight skirts, hot and bothered and always ready to get down.

The irony is that while African Americans say they hate these false images, many unwittingly act them out in every sexual encounter they have. I observe black men and women "playing the role" every time I go to a party or a club. Black men strut by me with their shirts open to the navel, wearing pants so tight you can see the outline of their genitalia. Black women swish past me in snug dresses that push their breasts up and out, and that barely cover their behinds. If we saw these same characters in a Spike Lee film, we would assail him for plastering stereotypes on the movie screen.

"We are lost in the confusion of myths and fears of race and sex," writes Ntozake Shange in "Fore/Play," the foreword to the book *Black Erotica*. "To be a 'good' people, to be 'respectable' and 'worthy' citizens, we've had to combat the absurd phantasmagoric stereotypes about our sexuality, our lusts and loves to the extent that we disavow our own sensuality to each other. So now we speak to our desires for each other to each other in a language where our relationship to our bodies and desires lack dignity as well as nuance."

Alma, a client of mine, blamed black people's troubles on history and their own willing acceptance of distortions.

"You can't talk about African Americans and sexuality without discussing the real issue of freedom," Alma stressed. "We live in a racist world that inhibits our every move. This has everything to do with our sexuality. If you can't see yourself as a free individual who is fully entitled to give and receive pleasure, then how can you be free to express your sexuality openly and honestly? We accept what society dictates without recognizing all the inherent hypocrisies."

Americans have always been hypocritical about sex. They put on a Victorian facade while "lusting in their hearts" and fantasizing about glorious, wanton, uninhibited sex. They project their most "unacceptable" sexual fantasies on to black people, whom they suppose to be "animalistic" and "close to nature."

The persistence of sexual stereotypes can be seen any time you flip through a magazine, channel-surf, or check out movies at the local five-plex:

• In a Nike advertisement in several national magazines, an illustration entitled "Falling in Love in Six Acts" was used to depict different aspects of falling in love: lust, fear, euphoria, disgust, truth, and the finale. The ad featured five white women and one black woman—guess which one was used to personify lust? Under the black woman's photograph was the caption, "Lust isn't a sin, it's a necessity, for with lust as our guide, we imagine our bodies moving the way they were meant to move. We can do marathons with our feet, lift pounds with our arms, have stars in our eyes and do a tango."

• Many movies are little more than glorifications of black women's behinds—their gyrating hips and pulsating thighs fill the screen. In the Eddie Murphy movie *Boomerang*, Robin Givens was a siren in a three-piece suit and Eartha Kitt had the predictable role of seductress par excellence. Most black women's roles are little more than caricatures; if a woman isn't a mammie, nanny, or nursemaid, then she is a sultry lover with nothing else to do but lounge around on satin sheets and wait for her man to come home and make love to her. Few films portray the rich variety of black women's lives, bodies, and loves, or their frustrations, joys, and victories.

• The popular song "I Want to Sex You Up" conjures up the image of robotic love, certainly not caring and committed loving, and many rap lyrics are openly hostile and degrading to women. Yet black men and women dance to these songs and blast them on the radio as often as they can.

African Americans are so bombarded with sexual stereotypes that it can take a real force of will for an individual to shake off their influence and come up with his or her own definition of sexuality. Dr. Gail Wyatt, a California psychologist and sexuality researcher, studied therapy sessions with 300 couples for more than twelve years, and published the results of her study in the April 1992 issue of *Emerge* magazine. She found that black men who did not identify themselves as "studs" thought they weren't "normal," and black women felt they should want to be seductresses. "The therapeutic goal they wanted to achieve," said Wyatt, "was to act in certain ways that were consistent with the media's opinion of black sexuality."

Wyatt emphasized that many "African Americans, far from being the sex-crazed 'jungle bunnies' that often spring into white Americans' minds, are fairly conservative about sex. What black men and women have done is accept someone else's notion of what black sexuality is and isn't. The worst part is how some black men and women decide to play out their sexual desires, never really finding effective measures of fulfilling physical pleasure."

Indeed, sexual stereotypes are so pervasive that they often elicit two extreme and opposing reactions. While some African Americans play up their sexuality by wearing revealing clothes and having multiple partners, others (the "conservative" group Wyatt mentioned) dress almost monastically, buttoned up to their chins, wearing loose shapeless garb that reveals nothing, seemingly denying that they have any sexual identity whatsoever. By personifying piety, they seek to show that they are impervious to sexual stereotypes, as resistant as Teflon to the demeaning images society tries to inflict on blacks.

Yet rebelling against stereotypes is not the same as being free of them. It is important for each black man and woman to accept that he or she is a sexual being with wants and desires like everyone else—to "own one's sexuality," as therapists often say. Acknowledgment, understanding, and ultimate enjoyment of sexuality depends upon internalizing the idea that sexuality is a vital part of being. An individual must believe it's okay to be sexual, and not allow sex to be defined by the narrow stereotypes foisted on black people by the larger society.

The Hunter and the Huntress

Because sexual images dominate our national landscape, sex becomes a disproportionate focus of many relationships; paradoxically, this prevents many black men and women from having satisfying sexual experiences.

Instead of revealing all of their facets, people often use sexuality to demonstrate their greatness, strength, desirability, and caring. Through their sexuality they seek the nurturance, attention, and affirmation to which they feel entitled. People who are "gender-confused"—imbalanced in their masculine and feminine sides—often use sex to prove that they are "real men" or "real women."

One well-experienced woman told me once that you are either the hunter or the huntress, and the main goal is capturing the game. She said she got tired of being hunted down and decided to take matters into her own hands. "Sometimes you have to seize power because the brothers try to take it all. You got to let them know that this is your stuff." She believed that by transforming herself into a "huntress," she was turning history and myth to her own advantage: if men were going to try to use her as a sex object, she may as well become the huntress, finding sex objects of her own.

Becoming the huntress is also a defiant reaction to a repressive cultural stereotype: if black women express sexual desires, they are "whores." Little girls are told to "close those legs and keep that dress down," while boys have no such restrictions on their clothing and behavior, and when they become teenagers are told to get as much as they can, wherever they can.

Shame about sex is deeply rooted in black women's history, religious upbringing, and social conditioning. Although most African cultures accept sexuality as a natural and pleasurable part of life, Africans who were brought to this country as slaves found this attitude brutally altered. Women started out in this culture as breeders and vessels of pleasure for any man who could take them; generations later, many women still feel shame about their sexual history and conflicted about distinguishing "sex object" from wholesome sexuality.

Black women are so stereotyped as sex objects that sometimes, no matter how conservatively dressed they are, black women in public places are sometimes treated like prostitutes. I saw evidence of this one summer when some female friends and I went by train from New Haven, Connecticut, to Southampton, Long Island, to attend a concert. A white man who looked like a business executive pulled out a twenty-dollar bill from his pocket and suggestively held it out to one of my friends, a Harvard graduate who worked for one of America's leading corporations, as if she were there on the train to "do business." We were all aghast at his behavior. Nothing in her conduct or dress could possibly have given him that idea; only the color of her skin could have marked her in his eyes as "prey."

Dr. Gwendolyn Goldsby Grant, a psychologist and advice columnist for *Essence* magazine, used the phrase "penis politics" to describe the male approach to sexuality. She said that women have to accept that men are at the opposite end of the spectrum when it comes to sexual experience and sexual response. A man "will make many of his sexual decisions strictly based on his penis and his erection, nothing else," she said. "It's what I call using his little head instead of his big head."

Researchers have documented how men in this culture are socialized to be sexual aggressors and to compartmentalize their partners depending upon the need of the moment. If this is true for white men, let's imagine for a minute how this pattern is manifested by black men. As we discussed in chapter 4, many black men spend their entire existence trying to define and defend their masculinity. So it would be only natural for them to take the common male sexual pattern to an extreme. For some black men who have found no other outlets for power in this society, the only arena in which they can display masculine potency is sexual prowess and conquests. And the only people over whom they can exert power are their own woman (or women) and children.

When black women complain about black men always "trying to get over," they need to understand that this behavior is the result of men's shaky sense of masculinity. A "groin connection" is a safe one for a black man. It's almost as if he is thinking, "If society says I'm a stud, let's see how good at this I can be." In doing so, he is reacting to what sociologist Robert Staples calls white society's "attempt to emasculate black men." Staples believes that white society is motivated by fear of the black man's sexual power. In his book *Black Masculinity: The Black Man's Role in American Society,* Staples says the white man "fears that as the black man attains a bedroom equality, he will gain political and economic equality as well."

Relating below the belt also allays the black man's sense of vulnerability toward expressing true feeling. He can also use sex to anesthetize the pain and hurts that come from living in this society.

Men do not acknowledge, of course, that they use sex to prove their masculinity, to avoid discussing feelings, or to anesthetize their pain. When a woman complains that she wants a man to disclose his feelings, he commonly turns the spotlight on what's wrong with *her.* "What's wrong with you? Didn't I take you skiing? Didn't we try that new French restaurant?" What he's really saying is, "Take what I feel I can give you, baby, but don't ask for a part of my heart."

Sexual Healing

For some men, sex is the only way they know to allow themselves some tenderness. Perhaps they have a deep memory of some cuddling they got as children and they want to nestle into that warm feeling again.

I know many black men who run to women to make them feel better after some major romantic loss, rejection, or frustration. By becoming sexual, they somehow believe they can heal emotional wounds. One man told me that after breaking up with one woman, he always runs the very next day to another woman; if he can get her to make love to him, he knows he can feel better about himself. The good feelings from sex, he believes, will protect him from feeling any of the pain that comes when life seems unfair.

Many black men who feel entitled to "good mothering" believe that the act of lovemaking supplies them with their need to hold and be held. A male caller to my radio show said that he was sick and tired of black men whining all the time about getting their emotional needs met.

"The brothers need to get off the tits and grow up," he said. By saying that men had become too dependent upon women for tenderness through sexuality, he was urging men to take more responsibility for getting their lives together—for finding other positive ways of dealing with life's ills.

Sexual Control

Controlling black women is a way that some black men can give a part of themselves without undue risk, while still getting the payoff of power. A friend of mine describes it as "not taking your heart into every bed." This attitude reflects a message many black boys hear: "You can screw all you want. Just don't let her get your nose open." Translation: "If you show you care, she has power over you." Sex and caring are distinctly different things for many black men.

A man can use sex for immediate gratification in a society where there are few rewards for being a black male. Sex is a weapon, a carrot, an instrument of control. Listen to Maurice, a single, divorced stockbroker who has made a career of using sexuality as a means of affirming himself and controlling the women in his life. Maurice told me, with utter conviction, that being a connoisseur of women meant "manliness" to him.

AUDREY: Now, you mentioned something a moment ago that had me curious. You talked about most of the women being nice girls, kind of innocent. And I started thinking about it. I was trying to get a sense of what one of those women in the "nice" category would be like. I don't mean what would she look like physically, but what's the difference between "the nice girls" and one of the ladies who's outside your grasp?

MAURICE: Normally the nice girls have come up very strictly raised.

AUDREY: Strictly raised?

MAURICE: They spent most of their younger life in school and college. They didn't get to party much. They stayed pretty straitlaced. Not a lot of alcohol, no drugs, no anything, you know. When I mention some of the Motown records, they've never heard of them.

AUDREY: They were not exposed to the "hip" life?

MAURICE: Yes, I know several girls like that. Something will come on the radio and I'll say, "Who is that?" And they will be right in my age range, and they have no idea.

AUDREY: They have no idea!

MAURICE: No idea. It could be someone like the Supremes. I say, "God, what did you do coming up?" She'd say, "Well, I just didn't listen to music. I was in school. I was doing this, I was doing that."

Their sex life is like, missionary. When you tell them, "What about this?" it's like, "Wow!" This is brand new for them. They could be putting on a show, but most of the time I believe they do not know much about sexual pleasures.

AUDREY: So they've not experienced various forms of sexual play?

MAURICE: Right. What I call this is like—not a sheltered life, but just kind of limited in those areas. Now, bookwise they may be experienced.

AUDREY: So it sounds like you like women who are somewhat inexperienced sexually?

MAURICE: Right. That's another thing. A lot of them have met a guy and maybe dated him from college or some of them may have gotten married to the guy that they went with in college. They stayed with him until just the last year or two and now they have gotten a divorce. They are free and ready to get out there, but they are like thirty-five or forty years old and inexperienced.

AUDREY: With very little experience.

MAURICE: Right. And then when they meet someone like myself they say, "Wow, this is a lot of fun. For all these years I haven't really had any fun, in this respect. I mean, I've gone here, I've gone there, I've traveled a lot. But now I'm actually having some fun. I'm being able to talk freely with a man, that I've never been able to talk freely with before. And he's not belittling me or thinking that I'm a slut because I enjoy sex."

AUDREY: Have you ever met one woman who went from being very conservative—the Goody Two-shoes type—to being so turned on by you sexually that she became really creative, even kinky?

MAURICE: Yes. They kind of get a little loose sometimes. They have never gotten so far out there sexually that it went past "way-outness." Some simply came around to what I wanted them to be sexually.

Maurice did not want to accept that he used sex as a means of control—that he needed to be dominant and aggressive with women to shore up his masculinity and prove that he was desirable. He made women feel "safe" about exploring their sexual fantasies, then hurt them by casually moving on to the next woman, the next ego-building experience.

Is It Love or Lust?

Some women in one of my support groups gasped when Geneva, a single woman, declared that she loved sex and had real problems being without it. Sex is a subject rarely discussed by African-American women in groups. Geneva clearly defined her femininity by the sexual action she was able to receive, and like some of the men she knew, took note of how often she "got it" and how long an interval there was in between "doing it" and who the "great lovers" really were. Here's a sample of the candor with which Geneva shared her experiences—and embarrassed some of the sisters in the group.

GENEVA: Girls, let me tell you, I had the best "stuff" I've ever had last Saturday with a man I'll call Wes. We met at a golf tournament and hit it right off and began going out socially to movies, dinner, and things.

REGINA: I can't believe you are talking about another man again. Didn't you just break up with one two months ago? Don't you ever take time off? Sex isn't everything, girl.

GENEVA: I know it's not everything, but to me it's what I need to feel good, and this new man knows how to make me feel like a natural woman.

REGINA: I wish I had a man in my life who just wanted to make me feel like a lady. All the ones I've ever had were interested in what I could do for them, so they could find themselves and reach their full potential.

GENEVA: Well, I don't worry about those issues with men. All I know is that I don't do well without them and until I can find one who wants to settle down, all of them are going to make me feel like a "lady." I got a "fall collection" of men and a "summer collection." This way I don't find myself experiencing any "dry seasons."

A number of the women in the group were angered by Geneva's attitude. They asked, "Why do you feel you 'need' a man? Where is your self-esteem? Your self-confidence? Your sense of identity as an independent black woman?" Some felt she was letting them down by presenting a side of the social world that few women got to see.

The dilemma for black women is that if they are open about sexuality they fear they will reinforce the myth of the "hot, sultry" black woman, and if they accept celibacy or self-pleasuring they are seen as gay or as man haters. Because Geneva rejected the cultural norm and created what worked best for her, she was often rejected by the other women in the group. Some said they felt disgusted by her, some said they felt sorry for her sense of neediness. But others envied her risk taking and pleasure seeking.

In some ways, lust is more familiar than love in American society. Movies, TV, magazines, even commercials virtually provide roadmaps to lust: this is how you move, put on makeup, what you wear. Love is still more of an adventure, a risk, a mystery. There are no roadmaps for love. For many it is the scariest uncharted territory in the world.

There is genuine confusion in this country about the difference between love and lust. Until you know that difference, you can cause yourself a lot of needless pain and anxiety.

Lust generally comes first. It's a feeling of intense, unrestrained sexual craving that seems to take one over. It's overwhelming and can be addictive. The feeling can be so strong that the uninitiated feel that this certainly must be love. What they are ignoring is that this same feeling can disappear as quickly as it arrives.

Love doesn't go away so fast. However, it can take months and years to develop. Love can be passionate, but the stress is more on a partner's emotional well-being and on the relationship as a whole. A loving union is characterized by respect, trust, emotional sharing of feelings, commitment, and responsibility toward each other. This feeling also requires work and nurturance, while lust takes on a power of its own. Love doesn't necessarily feel as intense as lust, but it's the healthier foundation for a lasting relationship. It's not always easy to convince my African-American clients of this, however.

Grant, a twenty-eight-year-old accountant, is a member of one of my male-female support groups. One night he was very eager to tell us all about his new lady love. The group was confused at first when he said her name. For weeks, he had been telling us about Joan, a woman in his office whom he liked a great deal. We assumed he was talking about her, but soon it became clear that he was not.

"You folks don't understand," he said. "Joan is okay but she doesn't do anything for me physically. She's not my type. She looks all right, but you know she just doesn't do it for me. I don't get excited when I see her."

The woman he was "so turned on by" he had just met at a holiday party. She was in town visiting friends and they had spent a few evenings together. Based on these few evenings he had decided that she was the woman for him, even though he still cared for Joan. In fact, conversation with Joan was much easier and more satisfying than with his new lady—yet Joan did not fit his idealized picture of what his woman should look like.

"Is this lust or love?" the group challenged him. They took him to task for not giving Joan a chance, and for chasing after this other woman after just a few dates. Grant was agitated by their question; he truly thought he had found real love.

Sex as a Measuring Stick

Aaron and Dolores, a couple in their forties who had been married for less than a year, came in to see me about a sexual conflict. Aaron was troubled about his new wife's lack of interest in sex. They used to be passionately and erotically turned on to each other, he said. Socially, intellectually, and physically, they seemed to "fit." They enjoyed traveling to the shore and to a winter ski chalet, and had a great sex life. Recently, however, Dolores had gone from being a "four times a week lady" to a "four times a month" very tired woman. Aaron worried that she no longer loved him, and felt that the lack of sex was slowly eroding his confidence in his sexual performance abilities. He had been recently promoted to vice-president in his corporation and was under stress in this new role. Aaron believed that his wife "owed him" increased support now as he grappled with a new and difficult job assignment. Unfortunately, he decided that the only way she could demonstrate this support was in the sexual arena.

Aaron told Dolores, "I'm sick of you always being tired, having a headache, or having wet polish on your fingernails. When am I going to get some respect and be treated like a man?"

Dolores replied, "I try to be sensitive to your needs, Aaron, but I'm tired, overwhelmed with my own responsibilities. I'm overworked at the office, and since my mother got sick, she needs me constantly. I want to know why the sex we had last weekend wasn't enough attention for you, since you know how exhausted I am right now with all these family pressures."

Aaron and Dolores clearly felt emotionally abandoned by each other—a classic entitlement issue. They both felt entitled to know the other person was there for them, but were so needy and caught up in their own individual wishes that they could not identify what was really wrong between them. They were using sex as a measuring stick to assess what each was giving or getting; as a consequence both partners ended up feeling neglected and unloved.

As I got to know Aaron better, I learned that he had never received much attention and nurturance from his family of origin. He had always imagined that when he got married, he would at last get the attention he had always longed for. I helped him realize that this was a fantasy, not an assumption that Dolores had to live out. After grieving for the pains of his childhood, Aaron was eventually able to accept what Dolores had to give—and she responded gratefully to his more realistic and understanding approach. She felt less put-upon and spontaneously became more demonstrative toward him.

Sexual Urgency vs. Emotional Hunger

Among those who "buy into" the sexual stereotypes are men and women who claim they are so "highly sexed," they have to have sex every day. Dr. Grant calls their sexual antics the "Kentucky Fried Chicken" approach to sex.

"It's a piecemeal approach," she said. "A man will say I'm a leg man or a breast man and then you will hear a woman saying she's a bun woman. It's totally object-related sex. Black people treat sex like it's a homeostatic drive like hunger, where you have to have food to satisfy the drive. There are common sayings like, 'I'm going to go get me some' and 'I know what's wrong with you, you need some.' Black people act upon sexuality like it's a 'have to' when it really isn't. You don't have to have it."

While their sexual urge may feel physical, their sexual *urgency* stems more from their use of sex to gratify deep emotional hunger. A compulsion to have daily sex is generally a red flag—a sign that an individual is looking for the holding and coddling he or she lacked as a child. If two partners share this need, they complement each other perfectly and sex is likely not an issue. But if one partner believes sex is nice, and the other believes that the "nasty" is *really* nasty, they may be headed for collision.

Diana and Jesse had been married for twelve years when they came to me for counseling. Initially they told me that their problem was sex because this was the subject of most of their fights. Jesse was angry because Diana frequently rejected him. "She never initiates sex with me. It's always up to me or we wouldn't do it," he said. "I believe that she could go on for weeks or months without it if I didn't say anything."

Diana, on the other hand, thought his sexual desires excessive and told him so repeatedly. "He's like a baby whining all the time about why I don't love him and why I won't stroke his head or hold him all night. I am often exhausted by the time I hit the sheets and his obsession with sex drives me crazy."

"Diana talks about me whining," Jesse snapped, "but when our five-year-old son whines, she jumps no matter what he wants. What about me? What about *my* needs? That's what I want to know."

Recently Jesse began having an affair with a young woman who worked in his office. I believe he thought this would force Diana's hand and make her comply with his wishes at last. Of course, just the opposite happened. She was more furious than ever and vowed to put him out unless he got himself together.

Over the course of his therapy, Jesse eventually revealed that his desire for physical closeness was also an issue when he was a little boy. He often wanted his mother to sit and hold or rock him, but she rarely did. Either she was too tired or she shrugged him off, telling him, "Be a little man and go take care of yourself." Now Diana, like his mother, wanted him to resolve those needs himself and leave her alone.

I encouraged Jesse to remember how he had felt about not being touched, held, and played with enough as a toddler and child. At first he held back, but eventually murmured, "I was not allowed to cry much and if I whined I was told to 'shut up.' When I fell down I was told, 'Boys don't cry.' My mother used to say, 'I'm not going to pamper you. Sissies don't survive in the 'hood.' "

So many men long to express their feelings, but feel ashamed of them at the same time. Through sex they can access their tender side, but they feel angry about having to be dependent on women in order to feel it.

Jesse had difficulty allowing himself to express his feelings and accepting that I would really listen. He became impatient with the process and wanted his wife to make love to him "now." He had waited all his life for emotional exchange between him and his mother, why did he still have to wait?

When Jesse and I attempted to explore other ways besides sex for him to become emotionally intimate with Diana, he clammed up. It is much more difficult to express emotions than to express how many times a week one needs sex. Jesse kept track of how often he had sex, but could not remember the last time he and his wife shared an affectionate moment.

I had to increase Jesse's sessions to twice a week as he dealt with the immediate crisis of his failing marriage. We worked on his taking more responsibility for his emotional needs in the relationship. I eventually got Diana to come in after Jesse began to feel more whole inside himself. We worked on their expression of caring, emotional intimacy, and sexuality.

Diana was eager for more affection, but was uncomfortable with sexual behavior. Her family had taught her that sex was not for "nice" girls to enjoy—that only bad girls "did it" with passion. She said, "My mother always called sex the 'nasty.' I do not want to be thought of as a dirty woman." Intellectually, Diana realized that sex is an important and integral aspect of marriage, but it took time for her to integrate this awareness into her behavior. To help her get started, I encouraged her to start showing Jesse more affection, whether he invited her to or not. This also, of course, met Jesse's need for more loving touch.

In time, Jesse and Diana were able to stop playing tug-of-war and to enjoy a greater range of emotional and sexual expression. Jesse understood that he had been using sex to replace longed-for holding and acknowledgment that he had not had enough of as a child. And he got over his old-fashioned idea that if a woman loves her husband she will have sex whenever he wants her. As he explored other ways of achieving emotional intimacy, Diana felt less pressured and more responsive. She was also able to get in touch with her sexuality for the first time in her life. She discovered that the "nasty" can be very nice indeed!

What most men and women really want is closeness—emotional and sexual—with a responsible and responsive partner. Yet for black couples in particular, there are many psychological and social obstacles. Too often, sex is the only way they feel safe to express emotions without feeling that they are getting too dependent, *too* close. Sex becomes a route of exchange, a less risky way to give of oneself. "I give her sex, she's satisfied," said one client of mine. Yet sexual give-and-take is not equivalent to emotional sharing.

Women clients often admit to me that they give sex to get love; men clients confess that they pretend to give love in order to get sex. Both pretenses set up vicious cycles of disappointment and hurt. When relationships fail, defenses go back up, love games and power plays spring back into action, and people convince themselves that they are in control.

When many men (and some women) finally *do* commit to a relationship, they feel terror along with love. The comments of Roland, a thirty-five-year-old client, are typical: "I really want to be able to open my heart to Lena, but all my experience has taught me that the moment I do that and she's not there, I feel destroyed. If I open my heart, I want my woman to give me affection all the time. There's no room for 'half-stepping' with me."

Roland could not tolerate anything less than Lena's total attention. She was not "allowed" to be tired, to have a headache, to be distracted by a deadline at work, to be ill, to devote herself to a sick child. When she was not fully present for him, he felt neglected and aggrieved, and decided to pull back—to give her only "half" of his heart. This, he told me, was his way of "playing it safe."

When gender identity is not balanced, when a person does not feel comfortable with both the masculine and feminine sides, he or she feels it's impossible to open up and get close, and still survive. If, on the other hand, the masculine and feminine sides are balanced, or "blended," then a person does not have to depend exclusively on a partner for nurturance; one can nurture oneself.

When, through therapy, Roland began to get in touch with his feminine side, he was able to be more giving toward Lena. When she had menstrual cramps, he comforted her rather than feeling that her pain was a form of neglect of himself. The couple were less polarized because he was less polarized within himself. They could achieve a balanced unity—a capacity to collaborate toward the mutual goal of achieving "good loving."

Love has many faces; it will not look the same for everyone. When two people decide to build a partnership, they must discover together a definition of love that works for both of them. They must especially vow to assume less and be patient; issues developed over years will only subside with a great deal of time and effort. What partners need is a shared commitment to confront problems together and support each other's growth.

7

Giving Up Entitlement

It is important that we as a people remember to be responsible and responsive to ourselves. Rarely does a person say, "I choose" to be happy and take responsibility for his or her own happiness and love.

—MELVIN L. HARDY, JR.

We all know couples who have a "favorite" fight that goes on between them constantly. If you spend much time with them, you can almost follow the script. Why do couples become embroiled in the same arguments over and over again? Both usually fear that if they give up their position, they will be at their partner's mercy. Men often say that they don't want to be reduced to a "wimp"; women often tell me that they want to make sure they have "an equal say." What both partners really fear is being vulnerable and dealing with the anxiety of change. Even if they are both miserable and no one is ever declared the winner, at least they are on familiar territory.

When I see people invested in repeated, ruinous behavior, I invite them to contemplate the changes that would be possible if they both just gave up a little power. I know this isn't easy; the unknown is always scary. But to win in the long run, you must try to find a solution that lets both partners feel like winners.

Conflict is not always bad. Learning how to settle disagreements together can actually bring a couple closer together. If two people have repeated conflicts, it means only that they have not found a suitable solution together. On the other hand, if they rarely have arguments, it's an indication that they may be fearful of disagreements, and that one or both partners could be suffering in silence, even feeling victimized.

The ability to discuss and resolve conflicts without hostility helps to build compatibility and support loving connections. Conflict can help a person to grow because we learn many things about ourselves in the process of looking at our differences with a partner. Couples who can agree to disagree are also supporting each other. They spare each other the debilitating "You owe me" or "What have you done for me lately?"

For many black couples, "supportive conflict" is a difficult prospect because they are accustomed to expecting that every fight has a winner, and that establishing who is right is more important than resolving the conflict. To achieve a win-win status, both parties have to be confident in themselves, considerate of the other person's feelings, and willing to compromise.

The first step toward achieving a better relationship is attaining a greater understanding of oneself. I frequently remind people that taking an honest look at themselves is perhaps the most difficult thing they will ever do; truth-seeking takes openness, patience, and courage. This is especially true for African Americans, each of whom endures two struggles: the external struggle for economic and social survival in a racist society, and the internal struggle to maintain self-esteem, cultural identity, and gender identity. All too often the external struggle, though compelling, is also a convenient distraction from facing inner conflicts. The external struggle is less threatening because turning inward presents the risk of dredging up old issues that some believe are best left in the dark. But we can deal with these issues only by bringing them into the light.

In some instances, the process of self-discovery involves the pain of discussing potentially sad and shameful matters, such as anger and disappointment in a parent or caregiver. When Jim Vance, a well-known Washington television news anchor, finally entered therapy to deal with a drug dependency, he was able for the first time in his life to face rage against the uncles who had raised him. In "Life on the Edge," Vance confided in *Washingtonian* magazine reporter Barbara Matusow:

[My uncles always said] "Straighten up. Hold your head up. Stand up. Be a man . . . Never let 'em see you cry. Never show weakness . . ." My uncles were all Depression people. . . . They lived at a time before *Brown v. Board of Education*, when there were places they couldn't go and barriers they had to accept. They could remember when abusing blacks was Saturday-night sport. And all they were trying to do was prepare me for the world as it was in those days. Even though it was beginning to change, they knew I wasn't going to have it easy, and they wanted me to be ready. And I love them for that now. I didn't love them for it then.

Many individuals are so fearful of exposing their private psychic worlds that they put off addressing personal stumbling blocks until they are in tremendous pain or crisis. Even then, rarely do both partners together make the decision to go to a therapist. One question I always ask in the first interview is, "What brings you both here for counseling?" Nine out of ten times, someone will say, "I'm here because so-and-so said I needed to be here." This is a control statement. What it really means is: "Ain't nobody changing me. I am what I am and I am not about making any new decisions about what I will do with myself." The resistant partner is generally the one who is comfortable only in situations he or she can dominate. Therefore, this partner is more invested in being in control than in yielding to a shared power structure in the relationship.

Most couples who come to me do not want to hear that each partner must first look within. They think that either the other partner is the "problem partner," or that *together* they should reach some resolution to their problems. While one partner might be in greater need of insight, and while it is true that partners ultimately must work together, the starting point is still within each individual. Whatever past issues each brings to the relationship will eventually seep out in the way the partners interact. Therefore, it is imperative for both to become more aware of each's own behavior and how each responds to the other.

Developing this self-awareness is the single most critical step toward ending power struggles. This is especially true for African Americans whose power struggles often stem from feelings of entitlement. It can be painful to root out the sources of the entitlement—to hearken back to the gender messages one received in childhood, or to the continuing ache of feeling neglected by overwhelmed parents who could not meet their children's needs for nurturance, attention, and unconditional love. Daily life in a racist society may seem arduous enough without adding renewed awareness of stinging memories. Yet undertaking the work of self-discovery will pay off in higher self-esteem, a greater balance of one's masculine and feminine sides, and improved communication and problem solving with one's partner.

Often individuals are aware that there's tremendous sorrow inside them, yet from day to day they unconsciously develop ways to flee from what's inside. Once they do confront their inner selves, they often find pain—yet also healing. In therapy one day, a client of mine, Andrea, discussed, for the first time, the sadness she felt about her sporadic relationship with her father. His visits during her childhood were erratic, and often he disappointed her by canceling at the last minute. Bringing these feelings out was agonizing for her, for she did not want to feel disloyal to him, yet it was important that she do so because her relationship with her father had left her unable to trust men even into adult life.

Andrea left the session looking deeply drained. Yet when I saw her the following week, she looked better than I had seen her in a long time.

"This past week has been so intense," Andrea explained. "When I left your office last week, I felt so down that I didn't know whether I would even continue with therapy. I thought, What do I need all that pain for? But then a few days later, I was amazed to have a sudden feeling of peace. I really felt that bringing out all that stuff about my dad was healing—and that I'll even be able to open up some discussion with him about it and get our relationship back on track."

If you often wonder why you have such difficulties establishing harmony and balance with a loved one, take a critical look at some past experiences to determine how your approach might have caused tensions and misunderstandings. Following are some activities that can help you "look within."

The Self-Discovery Exercise

The following questions and situations can help you examine your own behaviors and their effect on how you relate to others. Give yourself time to reflect on each question, then write down your responses in a personal notebook. If you feel ready, discuss your answers with your partner (who ideally is also responding to the questions). Write down your reaction to the discussion. Finally, discuss with your partner your fantasies of what you believe it would be like to share personal power with each other.

- When you are in a discussion with your partner and he or she disagrees with you, how do you usually handle this different point of view? What do you do or say?
- When you agree to show up at a certain time to accompany your partner to a social event and you arrive late to the house, how do you react to your partner's anger? Don't rush and answer this one. Think about it first, then write out your answer.
- When your partner depends upon you to make all the important decisions, do you respond by taking care of them and making all the choices or do you feel resentful about their dependence on you?
- When you ask for attention and your partner does not respond, do you sulk or go out and do something your partner would find socially unacceptable, or do you discuss the matter openly by sharing your feelings?
- When your partner gets a promotion at his or her job, do you get excited, feel sad and envious, or try to work on your own career advancement efforts?
- When you are feeling blue or fearful about something, do you feel entitled to have your partner change your mood and "make your day?" How do you deal with this expectation when you feel moody and how do you react to your loved one if he or she does not comply?
- When your partner wants to spend money on an item that you feel is unnecessary, how do you react? Do you assert your power and support your displeasure with a recitation of your financial status? Or do you emotionally withdraw and later express your feelings through other, less direct means?
- When your partner is in crisis, do you respond with sensitivity, tenderness, and nurturing (without sexual overtones); do you try to understand what he or she is feeling, not what you are feeling in reaction to the problem?

- What are some typical situations that make you angry, fearful, defensive, or aggressive toward another? Write down as detailed an answer as you can.

After completing this exercise, people are often much clearer about their own and their partner's strengths and weaknesses. They are better able to identify situations or behaviors that set off reactions or bring on moods, and more likely to be sensitive to each other's particular needs. For example, when both partners are aware that a visit from Anton's mother is likely to make him tense, or that an overdrawn checking account brings back bitter memories of childhood debt and poverty for Carmella, then they can be better prepared to cope with or avoid these situations when they arise.

A married couple I worked with for some time complained bitterly to me about their poor communication skills. Nina said that Warren rarely talked to her or tried to find out what was going on in her life. This made her feel resentful and closed off from him. On the other hand, Warren felt that Nina never listened to anything he had to say. She would cut him off before he could finish a sentence, he said, making him feel that talking to her was a waste of time. Warren reacted by distancing; Nina responded by sulking.

By focusing solely on their partner's actions instead of examining their own, they became stuck in a cycle that was outer-directed instead of inner-directed. Nina had to learn to ask herself, "What am I doing that makes my husband reluctant to talk to me?" And Warren had to ask himself, "What about my behavior makes Nina feel so detached from me?"

Through the self-discovery exercise Nina and Warren began to realize how they each contributed to their troubles. Nina saw that she tended to be so defensive, she used interrupting Warren as a way to head off criticism she didn't think she could cope with. Warren realized that Nina's constant interruptions reminded him of his mother's similar conversation style. His mother was always so busy and overwhelmed, she tended to say to her son, "Hurry up, get to the point, I haven't got all day to hear your long story." By closing off, first to his mother and then to his wife, Warren attempted to salvage some of his dignity. These insights ultimately enabled Nina and Warren to speak more leisurely with each other, less defensively, and to at last feel safe enough to share the torrent of thoughts that each had kept bottled up inside.

Opening the Memory Bank

Confronting the past is a vital step in the journey toward self-discovery and inner security. Until an individual is ready to do this, real change cannot occur.

Because the past plays such a crucial role in how we as individuals see ourselves and the world, one's memory bank, which may have been closed for years, has to be opened and whatever comes out must be dealt with. This memory bank holds old messages that creep into our present transactions—messages that may stem from past separations or traumatic experiences. For example, I hear many black women of darker hue saying that the reason they don't have a man is that black men like only "yellow" women. If a woman truly believes this, then this assumption will come into play each time she meets a man, whether color is important to him or not. No doubt she heard negative comments about her color throughout her childhood, and has now decided that color is important to black men. In truth, we all know that this is not true for all black men. What she must do is go back in her memory bank to her earliest recollections to determine when she first heard negative messages about her color and how these comments made her feel. If she can bring herself to confront the messages and the context in which they were given, she has a better chance of letting go of her negative view of herself. Most people initially resist opening up the memory bank and exploring what is there, yet the insights they gain can lead to better self-understanding and improved relationships for the rest of one's life.

Once the memory bank is fully open and thoughts begin to flow freely, the individual will come face-to-face with some "unfinished business," a phrase psychologists use for behavior patterns and attitudes we take from our past into our present relationships with other people. Some people, for example, may uncover feelings about the death of a parent or caregiver, or shame about rape or incest, or mourning about their parents' divorce or failure to get married. These are all painful issues, yet if they are not uncovered they will continue to fester and poison current relationships.

To help individuals uncover old memories, I use an "unlayering" technique that could best be compared to peeling an onion; clients are urged to keep peeling off the layers of meaning and memory until the underlying cause is clearly in focus. Just as a child repeatedly asks "Why?" until he gets an answer he can understand and accept, adults must also ask themselves over and over again, "Why do I keep doing this?" "What am I getting out of this behavior?" When these questions are pushed to the limit, some clearer answers usually result.

Confronting Fear

Fear is the biggest stumbling block in the process of self-discovery for most of my clients, even those who are firmly committed to finding better ways to conduct their lives. What they fear most is change. The process of change, I often tell them, is like entering a dark room and searching for the switch. As you grope around in the darkness, you often fear what you cannot see; you wonder what is in the room, what you will discover when—and if—you ever find the switch. When you do find it, more often than not you discover that the room doesn't look scary at all; in fact, you feel good that you held on to your faith that you would find the light and that you managed to banish the darkness.

When I ask my clients what they fear most about honestly looking at themselves, I hear such responses as:

> "I don't know any other way to be. It's familiar and it's all I know."
> "I'll change when I see my partner making an effort, too."
> "My whole family acts this way. It's just the way we are."

Such remarks are indications that they are stalling or stuck, afraid to go any further. They are really trying to determine if they want to take on the difficult task of self-exploration, an experience that will surely cause anxiety, pain, and discomfort.

Often it is not only sadness that people fear discovering but also anger. They don't want to get in touch again with childhood betrayals or disappointments—and they are afraid that their anger will be so huge that they won't be able to handle it. Yet it is important to learn how to tolerate one's own anger—to see that anger need not be scary and can be managed. Anger does not have to be an obstacle on the pathway to change; rather, it can be an opportunity to get rid of self-pity and blaming.

It is holding on to anger that is dangerous. Repressed anger often gets expressed as sadness or depression, or gets displaced onto people or things. A man who gets so enraged by a glitch in his computer that he threatens to slam it onto the floor is not really angry at the machine but at his boss; a woman who yells at her dog after a fight with her husband is not really angry with the dog. Yet when the computer is in shards on the floor and the dog whimpers away with its tail between its legs, anger has been allowed to take an unfair toll. As I often tell my clients, "What's talked out is least likely to be acted out."

Anger can be a positive catalyst for change if it is a vehicle for expressing the real feelings that caused it. *Constructive* expression of anger should be a goal for every couple. When Nina and Warren, whom I mentioned earlier, were in therapy, Warren had to learn how to express his anger to Nina in a way that did not attack her, but which let her know the impact of her behavior on him and how he hoped their interaction would change: "Nina, yesterday you cut me off in the middle of my statement. If we are to work things out together, it is important for you to know that your interruptions anger me and leave me feeling that my opinion is not important to you."

Giving Up Defenses

Learning to relax defenses is essential to ending power struggles in relationships. If someone is getting too close, or making us feel uneasy, we often push the person away physically, or with harsh words and angry posturing. It can take weeks, months, or even years for some people to allow themselves to be less defensive and more open with their emotions, not only with others but also within themselves.

When individuals feel anxious about identifying with a less acceptable part of themselves, instead of taking ownership of it, they offset their discomfort by attributing these negative attitudes or behaviors to their partner. In this process, known as *projective identification*, partners are persecuted for something their mates don't like in themselves. For example, a wife who assails her husband for being closed emotionally might carp, "Why don't you be [why can't you be/why aren't you] more tender [more demonstrative/loving/caring]?" But she might discover that she is not demonstrative either. She focuses on his own shortcomings to distract attention from her own. And she feels that, in the name of love, her partner can and should endure her endless accusations.

A secure, comfortable, and trusting environment must be created so that partners can feel safe in relaxing defenses. I see this in my own practice. Clients watch me closely for consistency and reliability around time and schedules, and check out how thoroughly I follow through. Somehow my being reliable and nonaccusatory makes them feel safe, reassures them that their real needs will be addressed without shame or embarrassment. Of course, it also means that I can now help the client to let down some of those defenses so that we can get on with the important work of therapy.

If you and your partner are not in therapy but want to openly address some areas of disagreement, you must create a safe place and time in which you can both open up about real issues and neither will expect to be attacked. For example, keep the bedroom as a refuge for relaxation, rest, peace, and intimacy—and never let it be a battleground. Move disputes or heavy discussions into a neutral zone, such as a family room, backyard, or deck, or leave home altogether and take a walk in the park.

Choose times to talk when neither partner is overstressed or exhausted. For example, if your partner says something like, "Gee, I have had an exhausting day, and don't feel up to this right now," accept it and agree to talk at another time. What is the harm in waiting? You might be better off letting the tension die down a bit. I tell couples all the time to leave the heavy issues alone during the week, and wait until the weekend. It's a good idea to schedule a regular "talk time," such as every Saturday morning after breakfast or during a walk after church on Sunday. And give yourselves "time outs"—cooling-off times—when you need them.

How you begin a discussion sets the tone. "I want to talk and I want to do it now" is certainly not conducive to an honest exchange. This kind of opening salvo puts everyone on notice that a fight is about to begin, and is likely to arouse a defensive reaction. Yet couples continually use such lines to try to get their partner to communicate with them.

Examine your words, your tone, and your body language. If your hands are on your hips and you are yelling, your partner may decide to avoid conflict by disappearing, being silent, or walking away. He or she even may appear not to care. In reality, however, your partner may care deeply, and be trying to avoid an argument or hide feelings of vulnerability. And sometimes people just need more time and space in which to think things through.

Conversation Stoppers

Choosing your language carefully can help your partner relax defenses and express emotions freely and honestly. Beware, therefore, of the following conversation stoppers. They are sure to get you and your partner into conflict when you may simply be trying to have a discussion or reach an understanding.

CONVERSATION STOPPER	RECEIVED
"Didn't I tell you . . ."	Demanding
"If you don't . . . I don't know what I'll do."	Threatening
"If you really cared . . ."	Manipulating
"It's because you didn't . . ."	Blaming
"The trouble with you is . . ."	Analyzing
"All you men are/All you women expect to . . ."	Stereotyping
"Why did you go . . ."	Interrogating
"You make me sick when you . . ."	Shameful expression
"Let's forget it, you'll never see it my way."	Avoiding
"You remind me of my ex . . ."	Comparing
"I told you . . ."	Parental lecturing
"If you really loved me . . ."	Testing

Becoming familiar with conversation stoppers can help you stop these phrases at the tip of your tongue and substitute conversation continuers—phrases that keep conversation going.

"I really want you to know that . . ."
"I feel that . . ."
"What I think I hear you saying is . . ."
"I feel anxious when . . ."
"I feel worried when . . ."
"I love you; tell me what's bothering you . . ."

"It is important to me that . . ."
"I really want us to work this out together . . ."
"I perceive that you're telling me . . ."
"Let's agree to attack the problem, not each other . . ."

These conversation continuers are effective because they keep the responsibility on the speaker, rather than dumping it on the receiver. Thus they set up an atmosphere in which each individual can speak openly and be heard. Defensiveness is a surefire way to taint the atmosphere, but the following tips can help restore it.

1. Be sure to listen carefully to what is being said.
2. Get out of a reactive mode. Take some time to process what your partner is really saying to you.
3. Try for a moment to get in your partner's shoes, and see things from his or her vantage point.
4. Restate what your partner has said so that it is clear you understand what is being said. Then you won't waste time reacting to what you *think* was said. Ask your partner if your restatement is accurate. Do not go on to the next statement or issue until he or she feels correctly understood by you.
5. Make a promise to yourself that you will make a response only after you have thought carefully about what your partner is trying to communicate to you. Speak about what you were feeling while the person was talking to you, not what the person is doing wrong.
6. Remember to attack the issues, not the person.

These tips were helpful in Nina and Warren's discussion. In response to Warren's complaints about her interruptions, Nina was able to respond, "I get anxious sometimes when you want to talk, and my anxiety causes me to cut you off. I can appreciate how you feel, and your opinions really *do* matter to me. I will work on this. I can't promise I'll never interrupt you again, but I'll do my best to remember."

Rooting Out Your Entitlement Agenda

We are all products of our pasts, no matter how much effort we might put into our present-day lives. Understanding the profound impact of their childhood, adolescence, and early adulthood is a challenge many black men and women must undertake before they can determine why they can't get along. Following is an exercise I use to help individuals identify and unravel nagging issues that are holdovers from the past.

1. In a notebook or personal journal, write down four needs you felt went unfulfilled during your childhood or adolescence. For example, perhaps you wanted to be recognized for all your help in taking care of your siblings, or felt that your family did not really acknowledge how hard you worked for the school awards you received. Go back in age as far as you can remember.
2. Write down four things you wish your partner would do for you today. Be as specific as you can. For instance, perhaps you would like your partner to listen to you without interrupting, or to call you each day at work, or to cook a meal with you.
3. Compare the two lists you just made. You may be surprised by how closely tied they are. Examine how past and present wishes overlap. Do they indicate any assumptions regarding what you feel you are entitled to from a partner? Review the entitlement assumptions in chapter 3, then examine how the following list of "assumption busters" can help you to transform those assumptions into constructive affirmations.

ASSUMPTIONS	BUSTERS
If you loved me, you would . . .	Stop the fantasies about what you feel entitled to from someone else by working on those issues yourself. Have your relationship be about sharing love, not proving love.

ASSUMPTIONS

BUSTERS

I do everything for you, why can't you do everything for me . . .

Don't treat your relationship like a bank account; this will only cause conflict and problems. Thinking "you owe me now that I've given to you" will get neither of you what you want. "Measuring" love is confining; giving freely is more likely to inspire your partner to give more, too.

The world is unfair, my partner should know how difficult it is for me . . .

End the martyr thinking in your relationships. Believing the world is unfair and your partner must make things up to you puts an unfair load on another and leads to disappointment, pain, and anger. Focus on suffering, and you will suffer more. Focus on what you can do to make things better, and you create hope for yourself and your loved ones.

If you won't give me what I want, somebody else will . . .

Face the probability that if you always need someone in your life to give you something, you are struggling with "unfinished business" from the past that you are trying to resolve in your present relationship. Threatening that you will "find someone else" perpetuates the illusion that there's someone out there who can make up for past grievances. Focus on what you can do to create your own healing and joy.

When do I get mine?

Determine the difference between what you want and what you need. Then do some soul searching to

ASSUMPTIONS	BUSTERS
	discover if you are taking responsibility for these things yourself. Often what you insist you must have from others is something you could do for yourself.
What my parents didn't give me, I will get from you . . .	You can't make up for the past in the present. Your parents most likely did the best they could for you. What they didn't give you then, no one else can give you now. Think about what your partner can provide in your life, and what you can provide in return.
What I got from my parents, you better keep on giving me . . .	The *present* person in your life is not responsible for what your parents did for you. You are responsible for that yourself. Your partner is not your parent. Be open and realistic about what your partner can give you, while taking ultimate responsibility for yourself.

Grieving Your Losses

Some therapists refer to the bittersweet process of letting go of fantasies and unrealistic expectations as "grieving your losses." When people connect with issues from their past (such as lack of attention, abandonment, lack of intimacy), they often feel pain, anger, rage, and/or shame. For example, Mona, the woman discussed in chapter 6 who had been sexually violated as a child by her aunt's boyfriend, had to grieve the loss of her innocence and her sense of security and safety, and acknowledge her feelings of sadness and shame. Only then could she at last begin to trust men again and enjoy intimacy without anxiety. If she had not worked through these feelings, they would resurface again and again throughout her life, perhaps forever denying her a chance of love.

It is crucial to have support through this experience. Witnessing this display of emotion can be frightening for someone who may have no idea how to assist the partner through this rough passage. A pastor, therapist, close friend, or support group can also give you the encouragement and empathy you need.

What Your Partner Can't Give You

Not until you give up the fantasy that another person can make up for past losses can you accept what your partner *is* able to give. For example, a woman whose parents were very unaffectionate always wanted a mate who would be exquisitely sensitive to her thoughts, feelings, and needs. Yet she married a man who was not particularly intuitive, and she was constantly angry and frustrated that he could not magically know what she needed. She had to give up the notion that he would be the sensitive parent she had never had, and accept the responsibility to spell out for him what was on her mind—and do so without resentment. He would never be a mind-reader, but she could learn to appreciate that he was a faithful husband who did love her and wanted to please her.

Perhaps the hardest lesson to learn is that only parents can give unconditional love—and even they cannot always deliver. All other loving arrangements have conditions. Unfortunately, too many black couples expect that a relationship will recreate what was missing in the parent-child relationship. If they can join each other, while also accepting individual differences, each person will be less disappointed and better able to move toward a healthy, more fulfilling relationship.

Sometimes people fiercely resist the knowledge that no one can right past wrongs or fill childhood voids. They persist in putting their partner through hurt feelings, emotionally wrenching arguments, and even threats of abandonment as they try to get what they need in the way they want it. Such futile actions only result in sad and lonely men and women who keep searching and searching, keeping themselves from receiving what just might be available—albeit in a different form—if only they would open their eyes to see what their partner *is* able to deliver.

Sheila and Ray, married for ten years, sought counseling after their many fights over his long work hours and her constant need to have him physically close and involved in their home life. For as long as she could remember, Sheila had longed for intimacy—and had learned not to expect it. Both of her parents had abused alcohol to deal with their many social frustrations, and Sheila had spent her childhood making excuses for her parents' unavailability owing to illness, hangovers, or drinking binges. If only she had her own family, Sheila used to dream, she would finally have a partner who would be consistently there for her, someone she could depend on.

Ray, on the other hand, one of ten siblings, grew up with parents who were physically available but emotionally unexpressive, especially toward him. He wishes they could have had more special times as a family, and he especially longed to be more intimate with his mother. But she worked two jobs, and when she was home she was busy cooking and tending to the busy household. Ray's request for time alone with her was a luxury she felt she could not afford—and perhaps an emotional need she did not understand. Like many children in large families, Ray rarely received special attention from either parent.

When Sheila and Ray met after college, they felt that they were made for each other. Both wanted to be in a family where they could be loved, but neither thought about how unprepared they were to provide this experience for each other. They both had vast emotional wells in need of filling, and both thought they had finally found a savior.

Now their marriage was characterized by his long hours away from home and by her frustration at running the household by herself. She felt very much alone in the marriage and had constructed a routine of begging him to devote time to her and the children. Ray saw her begging as harassment and deeply resented her demands. The more harassed he felt, the later he stayed at work.

Ray used physical distance to manage his fear that emotional closeness could not be depended upon. He did not believe Sheila capable of providing real intimacy when he wanted it; Sheila actually did crave intimacy, but had learned to deny her needs. Sheila and Ray both feared emotional abandonment, but for different reasons.

Both Sheila and Ray had to learn that searching for what they feel entitled to from the past was a fruitless journey. Learning to give up the entitlements of the past was a painful lesson, fraught with loss. Yet in time they were surprised to discover it was actually liberating. They felt freed from their childhood "ghosts" when they could finally admit: "I cannot go back in time. I'm never going to have the type of loving father who is there for me all the time, or a mother who will unconditionally love and affirm me. I have to realize it's not going to happen, so why not accept what is truly available to me and see if I can make it work." Both partners realized they had to accept one another as they were, not as they wished them to be.

Sheila began to see that pressuring Ray to work fewer hours was getting her nowhere. If she wanted him to spend more time at home, she had to make home a more appealing place to be. She also came to recognize that part of the reason he was away from home so much was that he was committed to building a solid financial base for his family. It was not in Ray's nature to sit around the house on weekends while she gardened and cleaned up the house. Sheila stopped whining and concentrated on how to make the time they did have together more inviting. Ray was shocked when Sheila asked what he would like them to do together. He came up with a list, and much to her surprise there were several activities she could enjoy with him, including playing blackjack, trying out cross-country skiing, and planning a family reunion. They even went to a basketball game together, and he delighted in teaching her the intricacies of the game.

Even though the couple still had much work to do, this was an important step. Ray worked late much of the time, but Sheila now appreciated having a man who enjoyed being a good provider, and Ray no longer dreaded coming home.

Allowing Forgiveness

When you can accept that no one is perfect, you are on the road to learning the power of forgiveness. Forgiveness begins with oneself, then with one's past, and finally with one's partner.

Forgiveness of self can emerge through the self-awareness exercises earlier in this chapter. As you discover the motivations that have guided your actions, you can forgive yourself for past mistakes and begin to make more constructive and healthy decisions. For example, you can:

- Forgive the hurts you have caused your partner and find better ways to relate in the future.
- Forgive yourself for not spending more time with your children, and make sure to give them more attention from now on.

- Forgive yourself for getting discouraged too easily with relationships or job-seeking, and seek out support from others that can help you sustain your efforts.
- Forgive yourself for neglecting your parents, and plan to call or write them at least once a week.
- Forgive yourself for seeking solace in alcohol, and begin attending Alcoholics Anonymous meetings or an alcohol treatment program.
- Forgive yourself for being demanding of others without giving of yourself, and seek to balance your relationships more.

The more you grow to understand yourself, the more compassionately you can regard yourself and others.

Forgiveness of parents is linked to understanding and accepting *their* reality—*their* internal and external struggles. Perhaps they weren't exactly what their children wanted them to be; like everyone else, they were imperfect human beings with a combination of virtues and faults. It is only reasonable and fair, when contemplating one's parents, to consider their individual traits, their own upbringing, their economic and social circumstances, and their understanding of children's developmental needs.

It is important for us as a people to acknowledge the struggles that our parents faced, given the tremendous social and economic odds against them. It is healthy to extol them for doing the best they could do with who they were and what they had. Sometimes, when clients relate their parents' stories of perseverance, they also find themselves saying such things as:

"I doubt that they knew better when they called me a name."
"My parents had no other choice when they left me alone because they had to work two jobs."
"I'm sure my parents didn't mean to hit me when they were tired or frustrated."
"I know now that my parents didn't understand how painful it was for me to pull them apart when they were fighting."
"I believe my parents meant well when they sent me away to live with my grandparents. My parents could not manage their lives too well then, but they did not mean to abandon me."

These seemingly offhand statements spring from tremendous wells of pain and hurt. Admitting to the pain parents caused may seem almost disloyal. But you have the opportunity now, as an adult, to make different choices about how you want to conduct your life; you are not permanently imprisoned by your past. You can choose which of your parents' traits to emulate and which to reject. You can't pick your relatives, but you can make life-affirming choices about whom you wish to love. You don't have to imitate your parents or guardian's style of relating; you can develop your own. And you can discard the crutch of blaming parents or others in your life for what is not happening in your relationships. As an adult, your destiny is now up to you.

Forgiveness of your partner will emerge as you realize the part you play in your own unhappiness. Partners who both work on self-discovery can work toward developing mutual empathy, identifying and relating to each other's history and issues. A mutually empathetic couple is better equipped to handle emotional and social differences, reduce tensions, cope with letdowns, negotiate conflicts, and find creative solutions to problems. Mistakes seem less like life-threatening disasters and simple apologies, kisses, or hugs can take care of the little slights and misunderstandings that are always sure to develop.

Forgiveness is so important to renewed harmony, commitment, and change in one's partner that I spend a great deal of time guiding my clients around the impasse of past grievances.

One young couple, Rhonda and Dalton, came in to see me because Dalton was convinced that his wife was having an affair with one of her male friends, Hank. Dalton had found a note Hank had written to Rhonda, and was disturbed by the letter's intimate tone. Rhonda maintained that she had not been unfaithful and said that Hank was simply a friend in whom she confided—especially when she and Dalton were not getting along.

After several therapy sessions, I could see that Dalton was so focused on Rhonda's supposed affair that we could not move forward. He was so busy being a detective about the assumed wrongdoing that he couldn't connect with what his wife was really looking for: a warm intimate relationship with him.

I asked Rhonda to articulate for her husband what she felt she was missing in their marriage. Rhonda said, "I wish you would forget about the letter and forgive me for keeping it a secret. I love you and I just want more time with you. I promise you that I did not have an affair with Hank or anyone else. Please, just listen to what I'm saying."

Rhonda's willingness to ask for forgiveness helped Dalton to give up his intense focus on the "affair" so that they could get on with the important business of rebuilding their marriage.

The Forgiveness Tape

It is often difficult for partners to forgive each other face-to-face. To avoid the self-consciousness and embarrassment associated with forgiving, I often suggest that people make a tape-recorded message so that their partners can listen to what they have to say and contemplate its meaning before they have to face each other. If you decide to make a "forgiveness tape" for your partner or another loved one, consider some of the following issues that I often hear individuals complain about. For example, you might say that *I forgive you for being* . . .

- Impatient when I need to have your undivided attention.
- Too self-absorbed to realize that I have needs, too.
- So independent in thought that you forget to ask how I want to handle a problem or situation.
- So quick-tempered that you sometimes take my head off before I can finish my thoughts or sentences.
- So busy that you don't finish what you promise me you'll do.
- Different from what I expected.
- So conditioned to saying no that you really don't give enough thought to my ideas.

Ideally, each partner should make a tape. Their exchange can open the way to a realistic examination of what each is really capable of receiving from or doing for the other. Accepting that both parties will sometimes fail and disappoint helps to keep the forgiveness process an ongoing and natural part of their relationship.

Gender Blending:
A Step Toward Healthy Interdependence

As we discussed in chapter 2, early misperceptions of gender roles can cause a great deal of confusion in later life for both black men and black women. The result is that both sexes fall into rigidly defined gender roles. Many persist even while acknowledging that something about their behavior doesn't feel right. When I tell individuals that they need to become more aware of both sides of their personalities—the masculine and the feminine—they often look bewildered.

The confusion about gender for African Americans is a direct result of their learning at an early age to distrust the "feminine," or soft, side of the personality. Females are taught to fear that a more feminized behavioral approach will make them too vulnerable. Males are also taught that their soft side will make them vulnerable, not only in the world but to their own women as well.

Part of the solution to struggles around power is the acceptance that rigid roles such as *machismo* or superwoman keep partners from trusting each other. Some black women, for example, may have to admit that there may be some aggression in their style. They may have a strong need to be domineering and take charge because they feel deep within that if they don't, no one else will. There are also black women who pretend to be passive, so as not to upset the men in their lives. And there are black women who are afraid to show their dependent side for fear that no one will notice and provide the support they need. None of these positions provides a sense of true personal power. In facing themselves, black women will have to recognize that their need to be self-reliant is often more a need not to risk disappointment, abandonment, or losing control.

Black men have similar issues. For example, when they take a macho stance on an issue rather than admit that they might not have a ready answer or might be confused about something, they are denying themselves an opportunity for real expression.

Both men and women need to overcome their fear of the feminine so they can become more integrated within. This process of integration is what I call *gender blending*. The benefits are enormous because gender blending gives individuals the internal security needed to face their partner and the world more courageously and openly.

A man who accepts his soft feelings is a more well-rounded person and certainly not less masculine (as some fear). A black man who is willing to allow his sensitive, feminine side to be available for his loved ones can be more supportive and openly nurturing. At the same time, his masculine protective, tough, strong side still comes through. He has no need for *machismo* and covert control tactics. He is free with himself and thus more open with his lady.

A woman who accepts that she need not always take the lead and dominate a situation may at first feel a sense of powerlessness—even though she is only giving up her *excessive* power, not her intrinsic power as an individual. But once she gets used to allowing her feminine side to become as visible as her masculine side, she will realize that equality does not involve total vulnerability or weakness. She can speak out—but she must listen as well as speak; she can lead—but she must also follow or walk alongside her man.

Kwasi and Ebony, a couple we met in chapter 3, are an example of individuals who needed to be more gender-blended. Kwasi, whose mother relied on him to be the "man of the house," was so accustomed to being the responsible, take-charge member of the family that he needed to learn it was okay to be dependent sometimes, too. His wife, Ebony, had underdeveloped her masculine side. Even as an adult she had held on to her fantasies of being rocked on daddy's lap, and she needed to let go of being "daddy's baby" and become a more independent woman.

Gender blending was a breakthrough idea for Jamal and Tammy, the musician and engineer we met in chapter 4. Jamal resented his wife's greater job stability and earning power, but when he became less invested in tying his masculinity entirely to his work and more willing to allow the sensitive and supportive side of himself to emerge, their relationship became less tense and more mutually empathetic. And Tammy, who had to maintain a tough, decisive stance at work, was better able to step out of that role at home and relax into being a bit more dependent and collaborative with her partner.

Gender-Blending Exercise

To determine which aspects of your gender sides are well developed and which need to be strengthened, review the following chart. First examine column A, "Masculine Traits," and column B, "Feminine Traits," and check off those traits that you feel characterize you. Only check off those that are part of the personality style you believe you present to the world, not those you'd like to have. Then determine how many traits from the masculine and feminine sides are described in column C, "Gender-Blended Traits." This exercise can help you find out if you need more work integrating the two gender sides.

MASCULINE TRAITS	FEMININE TRAITS	GENDER-BLENDED TRAITS
___ Aggressive	___ Affectionate	___ Adaptable
___ Ambitious	___ Cheerful	___ Conscientious
___ Analytical	___ Passive	___ Assertive
___ Direct	___ Compassionate	___ Compassionate
___ Athletic	___ Nurturer	___ Sensitive
___ Competitive	___ Gentle	___ Strong
___ Defends own beliefs	___ Gullible	___ Nurturer
___ Dominant	___ Shy	___ Ambitious, takes the lead
___ Forceful	___ Soft-spoken	___ Interdependent
___ Has leadership qualities	___ Sympathetic	___ Cooperative with decisions
___ Independent	___ Tender, soft	___ Self-reliant
___ Makes decisions easily	___ Understanding	___ Takes risks
___ Self-reliant	___ Warm	___ Understanding
___ Opinionated	___ Yielding	___ Tender, soft
___ Takes risks	___ Dependent	___ Takes stand with others
___ Self-sufficient	___ Nonassertive	___ Expressive
___ Able to take a stand with others	___ Plays it safe	___ Sympathetic
	___ Relies upon others	___ Affectionate
	___ Follows others	
	___ Reluctant to take a stand with others	

When partners compare their lists, they may be surprised to see that they are more gender-blended than they expected—or that they really do tend more to either column A or column B, and have some work to do to achieve the balance of gender traits in column C. They can encourage and support each other toward developing that emotional equilibrium. They can also seek a seminar or weekend retreat for couples and work on these issues even more.

The Struggle to Blend

In order for couples to appreciate whom they are as individuals, manage their own needs, and appropriately define their masculine and feminine traits, separation and individuation must occur. I am not suggesting a physical separation here, but rather an awareness of the psychic differences that affect all individuals' consciousness of who they are and how they think, feel, and behave. Paradoxically, it is only through strengthening their individual identities that couples can blend into a cooperative and supportive unit. People in couples who try to read each other's mind, or who are unable to view things from each other's perspective, generally have difficulty achieving the balance needed to live cooperatively.

One day, a couple was creating a scene in the waiting room of my office. The receptionist buzzed and asked that I hurry out to stop them from fighting. When they saw me they looked a little sheepish, then walked in quietly and sat down.

Burt entered drinking a cup of coffee. He worked the evening shift as a conductor for Amtrak and came to my office straight from work. Ada taught high school English. They had been married only eighteen months. Both were in their thirties with no children.

The problem they presented was that Burt was incensed about Ada's continuing insensitivity to his requests that she keep the house clean. Burt resented "having" to tell Ada what to do, and Ada resented hearing it. The issue was not, I learned, *whether* the house should be clean; both were fairly tidy, organized people. Rather, they disagreed about what exactly "clean" meant. Burt had high and rigid standards, especially for kitchens.

"It drives me nuts to see a messy kitchen," he explained to me. "I like the floor mopped every day and the counters completely clear. Ada likes to keep fruits, rolls, mail, coupons, and all kinds of nonsense in baskets on the countertop. She even keeps all those little packets of mustard and duck sauce that come with Chinese take-out. Sometimes there's so much junk, the baskets can't hold it all and it spills over. Then there's no work space to actually cook." He turned to Ada and added sarcastically, "Isn't that the *point* of a kitchen, Ada—to have room for cooking? With all your clutter, it's a wonder I'm not starving to death."

Burt wasn't finished.

"And the refrigerator! God, you should see all the tiny little containers of leftovers Ada keeps in there. Amounts scarcely big enough to feed a mouse—and mice is exactly what we'll have, Ada, if you don't wipe up the crumbs around the toaster every day, like I keep telling you to."

Ada rolled her eyes.

"For God's sake, Burt, if the crumbs bother you, wipe them up."

"You know I don't like toast, Ada. I like my bread fresh and soft. *You're* the one who has to have toast. Oh, and those frozen toaster waffles. I don't know how you can eat those grainy things."

If I didn't interrupt this exchange, I felt we could spend the entire session debating the contents of their pantry.

"It sounds to me," I said, "like you're arguing over something much deeper than how the kitchen should look. Burt, why is it, do you think, that this issue is so important to you?"

"I grew up with my grandmother, mother, and aunt," Burt sighed. "Never knew my dad. I was the only male in the house and all the heavy household work fell to me. Those women always left the kitchen filthy and it was my job to clean it up. Of all the chores on my list, that's the one I always did last. I hated cleaning up after all those women. But when I tried to speak up about it, they said I was too outspoken. My grandma used to say, 'Boy, cleaning the kitchen is your job, so you just shut up about it.' "

Ada's childhood was quite a contrast. She and her two brothers lived with both of their parents until they divorced when she was twelve. The boys went to live with their father, and Ada lived with her mother, an indulgent woman who acted as though Ada could do no wrong. She encouraged Ada to do well in school and made few demands on her around the house.

I suspected that what attracted Burt to Ada was the possibility that she could be the mother he had always wanted. She was sensitive, attentive, attractive, organized, and responsible. Burt had always been frightened of being dependent on women, and he liked it that she was independent. Her style was refreshing, and she was drawn to him, too. Burt was unusual; she liked that he didn't mind household responsibility. His apartment was spotless, and he was good at grocery shopping. He was different from her brothers, who took no such responsibilities.

"I thought I was right about Burt," Ada said. "I can't believe what he is like now."

Burt took a gulp of his coffee. I felt that he was observing me closely to see if I was going to side with her. When I didn't, he seemed to relax a little more.

When couples are grappling with issues of control, I sometimes find it best to see each partner individually for three or four sessions so they can work on identity and gender issues by themselves. Sometimes individuals appreciate being able to work through sensitive issues alone with the therapist before revealing delicate information to their partners. I usually ask the partners which one would like to meet with me alone first. Much to my surprise, Burt volunteered.

Burt was so eager to see me, he was early for his appointment. He was anxious to talk about his needs and have someone listen to what he said. He was excited at the notion of someone's acknowledging his fears and struggles—not only those at home but those at work, too. Burt wanted someone to notice and understand why he wanted and needed to share the household power. At work, all he did all day was take orders, and Burt saw no prospects for job improvement any time soon. He began to see that he was insisting on power at home because he felt so powerless everywhere else. His exaggerated kitchen standards were his way of staking out territory and asking Ada to provide the kind of constant caring and support that he had always missed. He was finally able to talk about what it was like as a little boy growing up in a hostile environment, disclosing that his strict grandmother beat him and his aunt harassed him about getting good grades.

Burt came to admit that not every woman was out to get him. After the second visit, he said, "Maybe Ada isn't so bad after all." I noticed how excited he was about his individual sessions. He smiled bashfully, like a little boy. He felt accepted in a compassionate way for the man he was. He experienced a sense of being emotionally held by the therapist (a pseudo-parental figure). He did not want to let go of this experience! He wanted to put off rejoining Ada, wanting another session by himself. He was receiving the kind of emotional support he longed for and this helped him to relax his defenses. In his own awkward way, he was testing Ada to see if she cared enough to do what he asked.

Ada was confused by Burt's demands and unclear about how she could demonstrate her caring in a way that did not involve succumbing to his obsessive demands—or any demands at all, for that matter. She liked to do things the way she wished.

I explained to Ada that mutual sharing was a process they had to begin defining for themselves. I invited her to discover constructive ways to share power with Burt. She suggested that they work together on redecorating their living room, something that she had been planning to do on her own. Since financial problems were a major stress in their lives, I suggested that they also work together on developing a budget. But instead of tackling the entire thing at once, I suggested that they begin addressing the least sensitive areas (social, food, and clothing expenses), and work up to tackling more difficult areas such as credit card debt.

Burt's rebelliousness began to subside as Ada's need to be so super-responsible abated. As they both became comfortable with their "feminine energy," debating and discussing became less problematic and hostile.

Developing a Love Style of Interdependence

Many couples are in conflict because they are not able to sustain their own individuality while functioning interdependently with their partner. Other couples function too independently and are not connected enough. Look at the graph on the following page. Which of the three styles do you feel is the best emotional connection? Decide for yourself, then show the graph to your partner. Together, discuss:

1. Which style on the graph best depicts your relationship?
2. What do you see as the advantages and disadvantages of each style?
3. Would you like your own relationship to be more independent? More fused? More interdependent?
4. Do you feel that you have enough personal space in your relationship?

Extreme Independence

Interdependence

Fused Dependence

TYPES OF EMOTIONAL CONNECTIONS

5. Do you feel you have enough time together?
6. Are you able to view situations from your partner's perspective? Do you feel your partner can view situations from your perspective?
7. Do you feel that in an ideal relationship partners always agree? Can a couple disagree yet still have a strong relationship?

Let's take a look at how one couple applied these questions about interdependence to their own relationship. Arthur and Loretta had an ongoing argument that had been plaguing what was otherwise a good marriage. They had been married for five years and were the parents of one child. Both were committed to the marriage and, like many couples in good marriages, they shared strong religious beliefs. At a workshop for couples, they discussed their problem and showed the group how they achieved a solution that was acceptable to both.

Arthur hated the fact that Loretta liked to go out on some nights after work with Brenda, a friend of hers. She had known Brenda since long before she and Arthur were married, and had shared many social and personal experiences with her. But Arthur did not like her to go out with Brenda because he felt that going to clubs was not really appropriate for a married woman—especially when accompanied by a single girlfriend.

He couldn't understand how those evenings could be fun for Loretta, since Brenda was probably still hunting men and Loretta had found her man.

Loretta tried to make Arthur understand that having drinks with a girlfriend did not mean that they were out "hunting men." Meeting Brenda after work was a nice release and had nothing to do with Arthur.

"Loretta is being naïve about this," Arthur told the group. "She doesn't see Brenda like I do, nor does she see her the way any man would. Brenda is never with the same guy when I have seen her, and she is always on the make. I can't stand to see women act like this, but Loretta ignores it because Brenda is her friend. It bothers me because I know how men talk about women like Brenda and I don't want anyone to make those assumptions about my wife."

"To me it is a matter of trust," Loretta replied. "Arthur gets all hung up on what Brenda does with her life instead of trusting me to decide these things for myself. What Brenda does with her life is her business, not mine or Arthur's."

The trust issue was pivotal for Arthur because he believed it to be an essential ingredient in his marriage. He had to ask himself, "If I believe that trust is so important, how can I complain if my wife goes out sometimes with a girlfriend?" As Arthur and Loretta talked more about what was really bothering him, she realized that it was not her going out that bothered him, but worry that her reputation might be at stake since Brenda was such a well-known flirt. Together, the couple made some decisions that gave each a measure of comfort.

Arthur realized that he could not forbid his wife from going out with Brenda, but he could let her know that he preferred that they not go to certain places or stay out late. Loretta decided that having a drink or two after work with Brenda in a neighborhood pub, or having lunch or brunch, was a lot less threatening to Arthur than meeting her at popular dance and happy-hour clubs. Loretta also promised Arthur that she would keep reasonable hours when she went out, and would let him know when she would be home. She also appreciated his concern for her reputation and her safety and acknowledged that he wasn't really trying to control her. With this well-wrought compromise, both partners felt that they had won—and their marriage was not threatened by what was essentially a rather minor issue.

In chapter 8, we meet additional couples whose relationships flourished because they were able to develop interdependence—by giving each other space, pursuing common interests, fighting fairly, accepting each other's different styles, and achieving a balance of independent and shared purpose for committing to each other.

8

Working It Out

Serious relationships are built and sustained not only on heart-felt feelings but also on the degree to which partners are willing to "give up" a part of their lives to each other.

—HAKI R. MADHUBUTI

When I hear black men and women quibbling over the hopelessness of their relationships, I wish I could introduce them to some couples who have learned that there is every reason to be hopeful. These couples have worked through entitlement issues and gender-role confusion, have improved their communication, and are committed to building a passionate, loving relationship. Of course, they still struggle at times with certain issues; there is never a time when a couple can declare itself "done" with the need for problem solving, negotiation, and compromise. But these partners have learned to face themselves with honesty and openness, and are proud that they have risen to this challenge.

Chuck and Belinda:
Giving Each Other Space

When Belinda, a twenty-two-year-old graduate student, first called me, she said she didn't need "real" therapy, just a little talk to help her get through a "rough spot." When she showed up for our session, she was obviously in need of more than a "Band-Aid session." Chuck, her boyfriend of two years, had just broken up with her and Belinda was in tears during our entire session as she mourned her loss.

Chuck had meant everything to her, Belinda said. For the last two years, he was the center of her life—even to the point where she neglected her schoolwork and stopped seeing her friends. All she wanted was Chuck, but he thought she loved him *too* much. She couldn't understand why, since he said he loved her, he didn't want to be with her every possible second.

As the session drew to a close, Belinda admitted that she needed more time to work things through and would give therapy a try. After weeks of intensive work, she came in one day with a pleased smile. Chuck had called and, to her surprise, was willing to come in and talk with me. Now I would hear both sides of the story.

"I called it off with Belinda because I thought there was no hope," said Chuck, an engaging and earnest young man. "She gave me no room to breathe. She'd call me all day long, and search for me whenever I was out of her sight. She even tracked me down when I went to watch basketball games at my buddies' homes. Just to stay on her good side and not upset her, I started trying to guess what she was thinking so I wouldn't do anything that would bother her. And that would make me resent her even more. I couldn't make her understand that she was driving me bananas. Our relationship stopped being fun and turned into a burden. I loved her, but I felt suffocated.

"After a few months, though, I started to miss Belinda," Chuck continued. "She has so many good qualities. When she told me she was in therapy, I thought maybe we did have a chance after all. If she can become more confident in her identity, maybe she can give me some space and stop trying to control me."

Chuck obviously loved Belinda, yet she was so scared that he would leave her that she smothered him, pushing him away and fulfilling her own prophecy. When she discussed her childhood, the reasons for her behavior became apparent.

Belinda's mother was an insecure, lonely woman who clung to her daughter for support and companionship. She required Belinda to be with her constantly, a demand so stifling that eventually Belinda, like her mother, developed an aversion to being alone. As I described in chapter

2, a girl who never has a chance to separate from her mother has difficulty forging her own identity.

Belinda used Chuck to shore up her weaker "masculine side." At first Chuck found her "little girl" dependence appealing, but ultimately he chafed at her clinginess. Because he was reluctant to confront her, he felt he had no choice but to swallow his resentment and eventually end the relationship.

During therapy sessions together, Belinda and Chuck learned more about the need for separation and individuation, both for each individually and for their success as a couple. Belinda contacted her long-neglected friends, focused more on her schoolwork, and gave Chuck some breathing room. In turn, Chuck learned to speak up when something bothered him. By taking more responsibility for themselves, they were at last able to rejoin each other in a healthier way.

When each partner's masculine and feminine traits are more in balance, both partners have a stronger sense of inner security and clarity about their separateness as two distinct individuals. They feel confident in their ability to define their own needs and to express them without hesitation. That does not mean that they do not want others to be attentive, but rather that they accept that each person is ultimately responsible for his or her own life. Unlike entitlement thinking ("I need to find someone else to make my life better"), healthy individuation focuses on more appropriate and realistic expectations of a partner ("My happiness is ultimately up to me. No 'ideal' partner exists who can make up for past neglect or unhappiness and assure that I will never suffer again").

Juanita and Albert:
Equality and Cooperation

Juanita, age fifty-two, was a tall, striking divorcee with shortly cropped natural hair, very Afrocentric in her orientation and attire. After making many trips to Africa, she decided to open a boutique featuring distinctive African clothing. Word spread and soon Juanita developed a loyal clientele. Only two years after starting the business, Juanita leased a larger space and expanded the merchandise to include African artifacts and jewelry.

Although Juanita was a successful businesswoman, she was a dervish of restlessness, going from one diet program to the next, eating in lavish restaurants by herself, and traveling so often that even her travel agent commented on how Juanita always seemed so eager to leave town. Juanita came to see me because she felt lonely and isolated. Lately she had been suffering bouts of anxiety alternating with feelings of depression, or "the blues." She was also exhausted, since a recurring dream frequently awakened her in the middle of the night. In the dream, she was alone in an old abandoned house. She ran from room to room, searching for a door, but to her horror discovered that there was no way out.

We spent some time analyzing her dream. Juanita was struggling with the feeling of being trapped by her past, and was panicked by her loneliness. The dream seemed to represent her fear that her life would never change, that she would always feel so alone. This feeling had actually taken root in childhood. Although Juanita grew up in a two-parent childhood, her mother was the stronger, more dominant figure and always encouraged Juanita to be independent. They lived in a lily-white suburban area and Juanita was often disappointed to be the only black child in her class. Yet her mother dismissed her feelings, saying, "Just get good grades and take care of yourself. You're there to learn, and it doesn't matter that you're the only black kid."

In high school, Juanita began to rebel against her mother's rigid control, and became pregnant in her junior year. She eventually married her baby girl's father, but not long after they had a second daughter, they divorced. Juanita was determined never to marry again. She set out to prove that she did not need a man, that she could raise her children and build her business without help from anyone. She often said, "I don't need any man to make my life complete. He'd only complicate things and try to tell me what to do, and who needs that?"

Now, however, Juanita's children were grown and she found herself grappling with concerns common to many black single women: "Am I going to spend the rest of my life on my own? Why can't I find someone who will accept me the way I am? How can I stop feeling so overwhelmed?"

It would take us some time to work through these issues, but Juanita could get immediate relief in at least one area. For too long, she had been handling all of the business matters herself, and as her business grew, so did her level of stress. I suggested that she hire a business manager to relieve her of some administrative pressures. At first Juanita was skeptical: "How could anyone possibly understand this business as well as I do?" Eventually, however, she relented and hired Albert, a forty-seven-year-old black man who was highly responsible, a whiz with numbers, and a relaxed, enjoyable person to be around.

Juanita and I worked for well over a year on resolving her internalized sense of gender-role confusion. She began to gain insight into her excessive need to control, her fear of vulnerability, and her disappointment that her father had so passively yielded all of the family power to his wife. Juanita realized that she had disproportionately developed her masculine side, and had blocked her feminine energy. In time, she came to trust that she could continue to take care of herself, while also allowing her feminine traits to come into play.

Juanita's relationship with Albert unexpectedly supported this process. Now that he relieved much of her stress at work, she felt free at last to pursue her dream of branching out into a mail-order business. Frequently she and Albert stayed late at the store, poring over other stores' catalogues for ideas, drafting budgets and business plans, and deciding which merchandise was best suited to direct-mail marketing. It was the first time in Juanita's life—and in Al's—that they had collaborated as equals with a member of the opposite sex.

Since Albert had recently become divorced from his second wife, he was in no great hurry to go home after these late-night brainstorming sessions, and he wasn't interested in dating, either. Albert felt little hope that he would ever find a good relationship. His own parents' troubled union had taught him as a child that relationships often offer more pain than comfort. To the community, Albert's parents had presented the image of a contented pair, but at home they slept in separate bedrooms and rarely spoke to each other. In both of Albert's marriages, he had felt so wary of the potential pain of marriage that he was distant with his wives, who in turn lashed out in frustration. He feared repeating those experiences. Furthermore, like Juanita, he was turned off by the dating games in which many of his single friends were involved. He much preferred to develop his friendship with Juanita. Not only were they both interested in business, they also laughed a lot and respected each other's ideas.

Slowly and naturally, Albert and Juanita's friendship began to expand beyond the store. They started going to movies, eating out, socializing with friends. The cooperative way they co-led the business extended to their personal relationship, and the trust between them blossomed into a deep romantic intimacy.

Both partners were pleasantly surprised by the ease with which they got along. They kept waiting for typical problems or games to crop up, but their relationship continued to progress smoothly. Juanita's growth in therapy enabled her to open up to Albert without fearing that she would lose her personal strength. Her interdependent and cooperative style encouraged Albert to relax his own defenses and resist the impulse to distance when they disagreed.

People who see change as a process of giving in to another person often get stuck and become resistant. But achieving personal growth, through therapy or on one's own, can positively influence others in one's life and open the door to healthy interdependent relationships. By confronting the lessons of her past and learning to relax her excessive control, Juanita at last managed to find the door to freedom that had always eluded her in her dream.

Vernon and Emma: Avoiding the Knockout Punch

When I met Vernon and Emma at a church couples support group, they had recently celebrated their twenty-second anniversary and their youngest child had just gone off to college. They were enjoying their "empty nest" because suddenly they had plenty of time to do whatever they chose.

I could tell from some of their comments to the group that they had worked very hard to achieve the togetherness they so clearly enjoyed.

They did not hesitate to describe the trials and tribulations they had experienced over the years as real work—and the problem-solving abilities they had developed as their crowning achievement.

Their relationship had a rocky beginning. When they had a disagreement, Emma closed off from Vernon to such a degree that she would not speak to him for days or weeks on end.

"I was so shy, and so fearful of saying the wrong thing, that I decided it best to say nothing," Emma recalled.

Emma's silence drove Vernon crazy. He believed that every problem has a solution, and liked to talk things out. Yet here he was married to a woman who couldn't talk to him when she was angry. Vernon knew that this was a major stumbling block for them as a couple, so he devised a plan to help Emma see that "not talking" made things worse.

"Vernon reversed behaviors," explained Emma. "One day when we had an argument, he withdrew from me, and for days he wouldn't talk to me. He was very dramatic about it, too. This was a rude awakening for me because I could see what it was like when the shoe was on the other foot! When it really started getting to me he stopped, but he clearly had made his point."

The episode was a significant turning point in their relationship. They spoke into the night about the importance of developing better ways to solve their problems, and came up with a plan that helped them through many a crisis over the coming years.

"We decided to set aside Friday nights for the two of us to catch up with each other after the long week," Vernon said proudly. "To this day, we allow no one and nothing to interfere with this time. Our Friday-night discussions are open to anything either of us wants to bring up. Knowing that we have this time together makes an enormous difference. Nothing builds up inside; we have a built-in time for hashing things out."

The couple also said that their religious faith helped support their marriage. They went to church together every Sunday and believed firmly in the dictum, "What God has brought together, let no man put asunder."

Keeping a long-term relationship on solid ground is not easy even under the best of circumstances. But Vernon and Emma learned the secret to success early: it takes work, work, and then more work. Yet surely no labor has sweeter rewards.

Carlton and Melissa:
Separate Interests, Common Goals

Carlton and Melissa ran a booming interior-decorating business, and even Melissa credited much of their success to her husband's charming ways with women. He genuinely liked women and exuded such charm that some women clients actually came on to him right in front of Melissa. But Carlton let them know upfront that he loved and was devoted to his wife of five years, with whom he had a four-year-old son.

I met Carlton and Melissa at a church retreat for couples. It was refreshing to hear that both had been lucky enough to come from stable, fairly consistent family environments, with good parental models and a strong healthy sense of being accepted and loved unconditionally by their parents. This is relatively rare for most individuals to experience—no matter what their class or race. Such family support enables people to accept themselves and to be free of feelings of entitlement. Good parental models enhance children's ability to create loving relationships when they grow up. They firmly grasp the most important ingredient in that process: to assure partners that they are committed to relating in affirming ways and that no matter how difficult life may get, they are there for each other to work things through.

Before Carlton, Melissa had several unsuccessful relationships with men she described as womanizers, manipulators, or very temperamental. The last such relationship, with an abusive, possessive man, affected her most severely, leaving her emotionally and physically drained. After a year of counseling, she was finally able to break off with him, but she was so depleted that all of her energies went into recuperating. Only at the studio where Melissa studied modern dance did she find solace. From the moment the warm-up exercises began, all she concentrated on were the beat and flow of the music and the beauty of the movements.

By the time she met Carlton, Melissa thought that men like him did not really exist anymore. No wonder his datebook was bulging with women who would meet him anywhere, anytime. Yet despite the availability of countless women, Carlton was attracted to Melissa, a lovely woman who had clearly been so wounded that her defenses were up and seemingly impenetrable.

"Melissa was so quiet and reserved, I wasn't sure that she was even interested in me at first," Carlton reminisced. "Eventually she told me what she had been through and I understood better why she was holding back. I could see she had been hurt, and I was willing to wait a while to see if she would heal."

"I was surprised that Carlton was so patient with me," Melissa told me. "I knew women were all over him, and figured he would move on quickly when I told him I wasn't ready for anything too heavy. Much to my surprise, he kept in touch anyway and began inviting me out for friendly visits. He never pushed me."

Carlton and Melissa developed their friendship for two years, and sex never became an issue between them.

"He restored my faith in black men," smiled Melissa. "He always treated me like a lady and a human being. I liked that he was willing to stick with me even though I didn't want to have sex."

Carlton attributed his gentleness to his father's example. "Dad was always my best friend. He was sensitive and responsive, and I watched the way he interacted with Mom. I can still see them standing in the kitchen, playfully teasing each other. They had arguments for sure, but I always knew that they would make up. My mother didn't always take Dad seriously. She had a good education and a career, and she would tease him that if he didn't act right she could take care of herself."

Carlton was so enamored of the notion of marriage after witnessing his parents' happiness that he married at a very young age. "It lasted only one year. My first wife was insecure and needed to know where I was every step of the way. I hated it. We had it annulled. But even this bad experience never turned me off to the idea of trying again. I just knew that I could make it work with someone."

As a therapist, I found it interesting that Melissa and Carlton spent an enormous amount of time together, yet related as if they had just met for the first time. When I asked them how they handled disagreements, Melissa said, "We don't get into debates that we can't solve together."

Melissa and Carlton felt secure enough to allow each other to pursue independent goals as well as "couple goals." Melissa, for example, had always dreamed of deepening her knowledge of dance technique by studying at the Alvin Ailey School in New York. Carlton supported her decision to take a temporary leave from their business and to enroll in a six-month course of study that required her to spend four days a week in New York. Their three-day weekends together were all the sweeter since they shared her pleasure in pursuing her dream. And they knew their marriage was secure enough to withstand the time apart.

"I have faith in the loyalty of this marriage," said Carlton. "I'm enough of a man not to feel that my woman has to be an appendage of me. I guess I learned that from my parents. My mom often went on out-of-town trips with her friends, had her own interests. Not once did my father ever act offensive or hostile or try to control her. He respected that she was her own person. That's how I am with my wife. Melissa and I have separate interests, but common goals."

Melissa added, "Since we work together in the business, we almost *have* to have time away from each other. While I dance, Carlton sometimes goes fishing with our son."

"Men need to be more consistent with their relationships," Carlton said. "When you marry, you commit to a group, a unit. It's not all about you, you, you. Your wife is your anchor, not your property. We all need anchors, and it's got nothing to do with manhood."

Carlton smiled, and took his wife's hand.

"Melissa is my best friend, business partner, bowling partner, and travel companion. If people could look out for each other, speak honestly, and not be afraid to work out compromises, relationships would be stronger and the divisions between the sexes could be eliminated for the good of the family."

Epilogue: The Way to Good Loving

The romantic life of black men and women has been under a microscope since we came upon America's shores. For many years we have painstakingly and painfully attempted to cope with the battle for love and power, and still we seem to be using the same old solutions: blaming others, pretending there are no conflicts, adopting some other culture's solutions, or avoiding the romantic experience altogether. Yet none of these responses has the potential for correcting our problems. Worst of all, our families are still under stress and our children are crying out for ways to end all the pain, confusion, and emptiness.

African Americans must find a way together to change the circumstances that have produced two decades of children living in poverty, and another set of children who are living well but are weighed down with entitlement issues. I believe that being loved doesn't cost anything and that a sense of self-worth is the greatest gift you can give to an individual. Love and self-worth are possible whether one is born into a single- or two-parent household—the circumstances of one's birth do not preordain a lifestyle of disempowerment and struggle.

What is important is to provide each child with a stable, loving, and affirming community and home; only then will they have the opportunity to grow up with a healthy sense of themselves. If they grow up knowing that they are loved they will be able to give love with realistic expectations and few assumptions.

There is nothing sadder than people who have given up their individuality in exchange for love. That price is always too high to pay, no matter how appealing a love partner might seem. People who give up their personal power to a partner will take on the role of victim and end up questioning their own self-worth and rights as a human being.

I remember reading once that the eyes are the windows of the soul. So many times I've looked deep into a friend's or client's eyes and witnessed such intense sorrow and longing that they seemed to be silently crying within. Each one had hoped that someone else would heal their wounds, and they would be transformed into a complete and happier person. But because that other person failed to do so had left them profoundly disheartened. If they could only confront their own unrealistic expectations they would be able to acknowledge what their partner *can* give, and receive the love that *is* possible.

As blacks, we are up against awful inequalities in this society that make it difficult not to turn against ourselves and our loved ones. Yet we can no longer afford to become discouraged. We must develop a cultural worldview of what black love is—and not let ourselves be defined by traditional Eurocentric notions of romantic passion. Love of your neighbor, love of your family, and love of yourself all require the same qualities: patience, understanding, respect, trust, honesty, and a willingness to sacrifice for the good of the entire relationship.

We as African Americans have great personal power and the ability to be creative. Our ancestors knew how to make the most out of very little resources, and we must capitalize on that legacy. Love was never a resource we were short of; blacks have always had an abundance of caring and a profound sense of community. Collectively, black men and women need to recognize that we can decide whether to spend our time together in a confused state or in a loving one. We don't have to allow myths and stereotypes about ourselves and our relationships to determine the shape and texture of our future together.

Selected Bibliography

Books

Ansa, Tina McElroy. *Ugly Ways*. New York: Harcourt Brace, 1993.

Ali, Shahrazad. *The Blackman's Guide to Understanding the Blackwoman*. Philadelphia: Civilized Publications, 1989.

Aldridge, Delores P. *Black Male-Female Relationships: A Resource Book of Selected Materials*. Dubuque, Iowa: Kendall-Hunt, 1989.

Billingsley, Andrew. *Climbing Jacob's Ladder: The Future of the African-American Family*. New York: Simon & Schuster, 1993.

Carson, Ben S. *Gifted Hands: The Ben Carson Story*. New York: Harper Paperbacks, 1993.

Chapman, Audrey B. *Man Sharing: Dilemma or Choice?* New York: Morrow, 1986.

Cleage, Pearl. *Deals with the Devil: And Other Reasons to Riot*. New York: Ballantine, 1993.

Cooper, J. California. *In Search of Satisfaction*. New York: Doubleday, 1994.

Copage, Eric V. *Black Pearls: Daily Meditations, Affirmations, and Inspirations for African Americans*. New York: Morrow, 1993.

Edwards, Audrey. "Sleeping with the Enemy." In *Wild Women Don't Wear No Blues: Black Women Writers on Love, Men, and Sex*, edited by Marita Golden. New York: Doubleday, 1993.

Farmer, Steven. *The Wounded Male*. New York: Ballantine, 1992.

Gaylin, Willard. *Male Ego*. New York: Viking, 1992.

Hare, Nathan, and Julia Hare. *The Endangered Black Family*. San Francisco: The Black Think Tank, 1981.

Hughes, Langston. "Early Evening Quarrel," in *Selected Poems*. New York: Alfred A. Knopf Inc., 1942.

Hurston, Zora Neale. *Their Eyes Were Watching God*. New York: HarperCollins, 1990.

Madhubuti, Haki R. *Black Men: Obsolete, Single, Dangerous?: Essays in Discovery, Solution, and Hope*. Chicago: Third World Press, 1990.

McGoldrick, Monica, et al. *Women in Family: A Framework for Family Therapy.* New York: W. W. Norton, 1993.

McMillan, Terry. *Disappearing Acts.* New York: Simon & Schuster, 1989.

———. *Mama.* New York: Houghton Mifflin, 1987.

———. *Waiting to Exhale.* New York: Viking, 1992.

Secunda, Victoria. *Women and Their Fathers: The Sexual and Romantic Impact of the First Man in Your Life.* New York: Delacorte, 1992.

Shange, Ntozake. *for colored girls who have considered suicide/when the rainbow is enuf.* New York: Macmillan, 1977.

———. "Fore/Play," foreword to *Erotique Noire: Black Erotica.* Edited by Miriam DeCosta-Willis. New York: Doubleday, 1992.

Staples, Brent. *Parallel Time: Growing Up in Black and White.* New York: Pantheon Books, 1994.

Staples, Robert. *Black Masculinity: The Black Man's Role in American Society.* San Francisco: Black Scholars, 1982.

Steele, Shelby. *The Content of Our Character: A New Vision of Race in America.* New York: St. Martin's, 1990.

Vanzant, Iyanla. *Acts of Faith: Daily Meditations for People of Color.* New York: Fireside/Simon & Schuster, 1993.

Wallace, Michele. *Black Macho and the Myth of the Superwoman.* New York: Verso/Routledge, Chapman & Hall, 1990.

Walker, Alice. *Possessing the Secret of Joy.* New York: Harcourt Brace, 1992.

———. *The Color Purple.* New York: Harcourt Brace, 1982.

Periodicals

Baskerville, Dawn M. "The State of Matrimony." *Black Enterprise.* May 1992.

Britt, Donna. "What About the Sisters?" *The Washington Post.* February 2, 1992.

Franklin, Clyde W., III. "The Black Male-Female Conflict: Individually Caused and Culturally Nurtured." *Journal of Black Studies* 4, (1), 1980.

Ingrassia, Michele. "Endangered Family." *Newsweek.* August 1993.

Jones, Joy. "Why Are Black Women Scaring Off Their Men?" *The Washington Post.* September 1, 1991.

Matusow, Barbara. "Life on the Edge." *The Washingtonian.* July 1994.

Pittman, Frank. "Men and Their Mothers." *New Woman*. September 1993.

Powell, Kevin. "The Sexist in Me." *Essence*. September 1992.

Sharpe, Rochelle. "In the Labor Letter." *The Wall Street Journal*. February 8, 1994.

Smolowe, Jill. "Race and the O. J. Case. " *Time*. August 1, 1994.

South, Scott. "New Facts and Hot Stats from the Social Sciences: Men, Women, and Marriage." *Journal of Marriage and the Family*. 1993.

Wyatt, Gail. "Black Sexuality." *Emerge*. April 1992.

Index

Fourth World Studios

About the Author

Audrey B. Chapman is a nationally known figure in the area of male-female relationships. For nearly twenty years, through her work as a therapist in private practice, a radio talk show host, and frequent lecturer and workshop leader, she has helped men and women discover alternative solutions to the myriad problems resulting from changing roles and lifestyles. She has conducted seminars and training sessions on personal and office relations for Columbia University, Yale University, the Department of Health and Human Services, the United States Air Force, the United States Navy, the Congressional Black Caucus, the Library of Congress, the Department of Agriculture, the U.S. Federal Reserve Board, the National Council for Negro Women, the Smithsonian Institution, Delta Sigma Theta Sorority, New England Telephone Company, and many other national institutions and corporations.

Ms. Chapman has published many articles and received numerous awards for her work in mental health and leadership areas. She is host of the talk show *All About Love* on WHUR–FM radio and the author of *Man Sharing: Dilemma or Choice?* She had been interviewed by the *Wall Street Journal,* the *New York Times,* the *Washington Post, Savvy,*

Essence, Ebony, Jet, Redbook, and many other publications, and has appeared on such nationally televised shows as *Donahue, Oprah, Sally Jessy Raphael, 20/20*, and *Tony Brown's Journal*. Ms. Chapman is a member of the National Board of Certified Counselors, Inc., and the president of A. B. Chapman Associates, Inc.

Seminars with Audrey B. Chapman

Audrey B. Chapman's articles and books have been inspired by working with the thousands of singles, couples, and families who have attended and benefited from her "Good Loving" seminars. These weekend seminars have been conducted for religious, civic, education, business, and health organizations, and are nationally recognized as an effective approach to establishing healthy ways of relating among individuals, partners, and groups.

At a time in America when people of color need solutions to the myriad problems of relating, Chapman's seminars provide an opportunity to identify areas of stress points within our important relationships, while creating a safe and supportive environment in which to explore these issues.

Seminars are open to anyone who wishes to experience a rewarding weekend journey of honest sharing, and practical techniques that promote love that's wholesome, stable, and focused on commitment. Among the many topics discussed are:

- Ways to root out entitlement thinking
- Creating gender balance to stop power struggles

- Establishing a sense of inner strength to take into a partnership
- Finding ways to forgive and let go of past disappointments
- Effective ways to establish communication and negotiate win-win situations

Persons wishing to attend a "Good Loving" seminar are encouraged to schedule in advance by writing or calling:

A. B. Chapman Associates, Inc.
c/o Twosome's Training Institute for Relationships
1800 Diagonal Road, Suite 600
Alexandria, VA 22314
(703) 518-4186
(800) 579-6553